THE BOYS ON THE ROCK

THE BOYS ON THE ROCK

*LISTENING TO THE
VOICES OF THE HOMELESS*

WRITTEN AND ILLUSTRATED BY
JOANNE M. QUEENAN

Copyright © 2012 by Joanne M. Queenan.

Library of Congress Control Number: 2012911529
ISBN: Hardcover   978-1-4771-3363-7
              Softcover   978-1-4771-3362-0
              Ebook   978-1-4771-3364-4

All rights reserved. No part of this book may be reproduced or transmitted in any form or by any means, electronic or mechanical, including photocopying, recording, or by any information storage and retrieval system, without permission in writing from the copyright owner.

This book was printed in the United States of America.

To order additional copies of this book, contact:
Xlibris Corporation
1-888-795-4274
www.Xlibris.com
Orders@Xlibris.com
108624

CONTENTS

Acknowledgments 7

Part One

Segue to The Homeless 13
Why People Became Evicted And Homeless 33

Part Two

Carla 39
Jean 43
Monica 47
Joe 51
Turrell 53
Georgia 55
Antonio 57
Iris 59
Allen 63
Mitchell 67
Baby Mama 69
Kenneth 73
Big Boy 77
Genevieve 81
Andrew 85
Hefty Man 89
Cheri 93
Lorenzo 97

Part Three

"If You Lie, You Steal" 101
"I Learned To Not Write My Name On The Wall!" 105
"Almost, Miss Joanne, Almost!" 113
"The Boys On The Rock" 117
"When Everything Is Coming Your Way,
    You Are In The Wrong Lane." 123
The Preacher Man 127
"Not Only Is Life A Bitch But
    It Is Always Having Puppies." 131
"Life Is What Happens When You Are Making Plans" 135
One More Nightmare On Elm Street 139
With Eyes That See Around Corners 145

Part Four

Status Symbols 151
Today 153
Gorilla Warfare 157
Body Count 159
Titles 161
Hard Day In The Playpen 165
Thanksgiving In The Soup Kitchen 169
Battered Women's Shelter 171
The Donor 173

Part Five

Amen. Alleluia? 177

References 179

ACKNOWLEDGMENTS

My gratitude goes to Dr. Ronald Arundell, Dr. Nancy Fox, Carol Crawford, and my husband, Bob for technical assistance. The encouragement of my children Rusty and Colleen, grandson Kevin, friends Mary, Helen and Diane, and my past and present Women Writing for (a) Change and SIPS groups were the impetus and my cheering section of the project. But, especially, thanks to the people of the soup kitchen who allowed me to share their life and struggle with them.   jmq

"It's not what you look at that matters. It's what you see!"
Henry David Thoreau

Part One

SEGUE TO THE HOMELESS

Once Upon a Time . . . A cuddly twosome paid their tab and left the restaurant with arms curled around each other's waist. The mellow wine they enjoyed had left them feeling more together than ever. It had been warm and cozy inside with the walls lined with old books and disparate nick-knacks. It was like a cluttered cottage, more than a formal dining establishment.

The blast of cold air tightened their hold on each other. It was only a few steps to the side walk when they felt assaulted by a couple men who were hawking a homeless group's newspaper. The couple's luscious evening took an abrupt turn. "Move away!" He barked in a harsh sergeant's voice.

Somewhat startled by the mean reaction, the salesman coaxed, "Ah, come on. Can't you help a guy? It's just a buck for our newspaper!" He pulled the collar of his wrinkled, stained jacket tighter around his neck. The finger tips were missing from his gloves. "Go away! Not tonight!" the diner ordered and hustled his girl friend to his car. The two of them tumbled into the vehicle and with hearts thundering, both quickly locked their doors. They looked cautiously back to the restaurant but no one followed them. The vendors just stood in front where they had been and watched. The men looked to each other with quizzical expressions, shrugged and ambled to another possible customer.

In the emotion of the moment, the man did not notice there was a parking violation ticket on his windshield. He had parked over a crosswalk.

The couple was obviously fearful of the homeless vendors, but the facts of their suspicion say just the opposite, that those fellows are less apt to perpetrate a crime than a person with a residence. It may be human to be suspicious of a person different from us. And many agree that most homeless people have a "look"! That used up, down trodden look with a sad face, shaggy hair and sagging clothes. Following rules of safety makes good sense. Creating problems when there aren't any doesn't make better sense and improve human relations.

One can wish that if the couple had known what drove those men to have to sell newspapers they might have been more empathic and even if they didn't buy one, would have just said "no thanks" and moved on.

The Book's Raison d' Etre

So who are those people who wander in and out of our lives holding a tattered cardboard sign announcing their poverty and bad luck as we drive downtown or pause at the end of an expressway ramp? Do we check our car locks as we approach *them*? Do we refuse to look *them* in the eye and plainly feel uncomfortable? As a pedestrian do we rush by *them* and tighten our coats around us?

What does it take to compel a person to beg for basic needs? Reflecting back, or maybe in the moment, do we wish we knew the stories about what put them in those miserable circumstances?

For a number of years I worked in a soup Kitchen and met people of all ages and dispositions. Some of those folks had galvanizing personalities. Sometimes I would be so moved by something poignant that happened that I needed to write about it. Thus this collection of stories. Some of these stories evolve from people who were outside the social worker office, some of them were not homeless or were outside the neighborhood. The stories written here are how I experienced and perceived them.

This is a book of tales about people like the homeless or indigent people we see, the ones who make us squirm and feel on alert and their look of dejection sets off our fight or flight alarm. These are the behind the scenes stories about real men, women and children who came through a soup line in the inner city. They are survivors of destructive life experiences.

Significant details on all the key facts on the individuals described here have been changed to protect their privacy. At least half of them have "passed," as the locals say. This book isn't meant as an apology on homelessness and poverty; rather it is meant to put a personality and a face on some people who needed a soup kitchen with social services. Staff and the hearty volunteers who work in all the soup kitchens of our country, become privy to the situations that bring the people to the serving line. Perhaps after the reader hears their stories, they, too, will become as fond of these characters as we were. Core aspects in these persons' lives are meant to inform, sensitize and perhaps in some cases engage.

There are a few different approaches to the story telling here. Some are told in narrative form to capture a moment or describe the person. Like snap shots, others are one page or shorter poems or maybe a 17 syllable haiku to highlight a significant individual or incident.

What to Do! What to Do!

How can we help the obviously impoverished person who has been reduced to begging for a basic need, and still keep safe? How can we help and still not feed into any suspected addictions and still offer a smidgen of relief? Handing cash may not be the best idea. Though that is exactly what they want and need for whatever the reason.

Consider this. It is not an original suggestion but it is not too difficult to prepare a few bags of ready to eat food to hand to the needy person as we wait at a stop light? Include some fruit and something to drink. Or perhaps have a nearby restaurant or grocery gift card ready for a someone asking for food? Maybe attach a current coupon to double the value. In warm weather offer a bottle of water or in cold, hand them a pair of socks, earmuffs, gloves or hand warmers. A little imagination as to what could be helpful to a homeless person can result in gathering some helpful items one can carry in the car ready for such an opportunity. A card naming homeless resources doesn't really help his immediate need especially when he could cite them from memory.

A Peak Into The Card Board Box

Here is a thumbnail sketch of homeless persons' facts. In the last 15 years the homeless population has increased 150%. Because the Kitchen described here is in Cincinnati, I made a few correlations to the national average relating to homeless people. According to the Greater Cincinnati Coalition for the Homeless, in any given year, there are 3.5 million homeless people in the U. S. On any given night in America, 672,000 don't have a place to go home to. Every night in our city there are between 1,300 and 1,500 people without a safe, reliable place to lay their heads.

Nationally, men compose 51% of urban homeless people. In Cincinnati, it is 49%. Single women represent 17% nationally and in our town its 16%. The fastest growing group of people to become homeless are families. 31% of homeless are families. In Cincinnati 25% of homeless people are children. The next wave of new homeless will be young people leaving foster care and single mothers with children.

Whole families can be bound in poverty and lose their apartment or home. Nearly a third of homeless people are children. Some find challenges to access shelters or return to any type of permanency. An abused mother of a pubescent male whose options had been pared to nothing, needed to decide quickly what to do with her boy if she was to get help for the rest of her family. There wasn't a place for fathers with daughters or sons. Families can now stay together in particular programs that comprehensively try to reinstate or create stability for people without permanent living situations.

In our town 8% of the homeless are veterans. That is a portion of the 40% of total homeless who are veterans. In our city 60% of homeless people work at least part time. 80% of homeless people do not have health insurance. Their desperate on-edge lifestyle can exacerbate physical problems.

Homelessness is not an unique American problem. England's Lancet medical journal published a long term ten year study of 32,700 people in Denmark. Overall, psychiatric disorders were the most frequent diagnosis of homeless people and the study determined a shocking 58.2% men and 62.4% women had a mental illness. Substance abuse is next with 49% of men and 36.9% for women.

Getting a grip on a significant mental illness statistic is difficult but it is said to be 16% nationally for severe chronically ill. Some sources place it much higher. And in Cincinnati it is counted at 31%. In the US, there are 26% of homeless people with some form of drug or alcohol abuse. In Cincinnati, 30% are said to be alcohol dependent and 31.5% with a drug dependency.

African Americans, represent a disproportionate number in the homeless ranks. Nationally, 49% of homeless are African Americans. In Cincinnati, it is 68.5% for that group. Nationally, 35% of homeless are Caucasian and in our city, the statistic is 27%. In the mid 90's the soup Kitchen initially counted 85% of the people coming for services were African American.

Most homeless people do not have cars and have to walk wherever they need to go. If the person does have a car, more than 3 out of 10 people live out of it. Homeless people are victims of the weather which in our mid west region the needle tips to either extreme. To be forever in camping mode loses its aura quickly. When we feel unwell we flop on the couch or rest in bed. Homeless people are not allowed to loiter.

Most certainly the lives of these people live are hard and isolated. Suburban and rural homeless are disconnected to the larger group. Most often, it is an abrupt and strange experience that causes extreme embarrassment. But all homeless people, no matter where they are located, live with the uncertainty of how they will survive into tomorrow. Having a life plan might be asking too much.

What's So Special About The Soup Kitchen?

The soup Kitchen targeted hungry people who lived in Over the Rhine, one of the oldest neighborhoods in Cincinnati. It turned no one away unless they were intoxicated or threatening. True, some of the people who frequented the facility were there as a result of one or more mistakes that sent them spiraling into a whirlpool of loss and misery. But, some others had misfortune befall them like illness, injury, job loss and other catastrophies like fires or accidents. No one was ever charged for a service. They were never asked to sign in or give personal information in order to get a meal.

We intentionally did not invade privacy and did not require reservations as one soup kitchen I heard of. We'd try to learn everyone's names but do it in a casual way. When working one-on-one with a guest, my task as a social worker required more details.

Ours was a bare bones operation. The manager would plan well rounded, tasty meals and run the plant. The people were devoted to her. The menu would change in response to a substantial donation that was delivered unannounced. The staff were people from the neighborhood.

We were located in the basement of a county building but we all tried to make the environment as comfortable as we reasonably could. The kitchen opened from 9:30 am until noon and from 1pm until 3pm Monday through Thursday. First, people met in the back room for coffee and day old donuts. Always they had room for the big meal beginning at 10:00 am. Volunteers worked two steady hours serving food on each week day. Fridays we opened at the same time and closed at noon, spending the afternoon scrubbing the place. Other kitchens were just open for the meal and on specific days of the week. We were open holidays even if they were on a week-end.

There were only caged windows in the front hall. The men had only one toilet and one for the women. The City gave regulatory exception to soup kitchens. Certain Board of Health standards were maintained. The place was painted brightly and kept clean.

We had a separate kiddy corner where little ones could eat and play with a care provider watching them while their parents got a break to eat with grown-ups. Grade school children were not encouraged as they should be in school. In fact, there was a relationship with the local elementary social worker to come and check for truancy. There was an after school feeding program for elementary children which was a collaborative effort with another agency and other funding sources.

Most of the years I was on staff, we were open on holidays. Even Christmas, New Years and Thanksgiving because restaurants downtown were closed and our customers needed to have a place to eat. As time went on and options expanded in town, it was not open on all the holidays. Later on, the place closed for a week in the summer for a staff vacation.

The method of counting who came to dinner was primitive but efficient. Guests were given a plastic chip as they entered the dining room. They dropped it in a jug as they picked up their tray. The chips were counted later.

We had programming over and above the meals. Ours was the first kitchen in town with a social worker. As such I was able to sit quietly with a person in need. It was easy to give them my full attention because they were fascinating people with gripping stories. The personalities of our customers were unique, like they were lit in neon lights. You couldn't help but be attracted to some of them. Conversely, if someone was not nearly as lovable, the closeness of quarters brought you closer than you would have liked.

The founder and director was a version of activist Dorothy Day. She almost single handedly managed the fund raising, kept oversight on the operations of the kitchen and office, produced the newsletter to donors and kept the mission alive before the community. One time I wrote that the place appeared to be designed by the Marquis de Saud. Not meaning to hurt her, I learned I offended her who devoted her entire life to its existence. But it was a cellar, a place with rock whitewashed walls, narrow walk ways and one thing I missed were windows. When you consider the accomplishment of the start up and over time, underwriting a fifteen year old operation that fed at over 17,000 meals a year, Namaste! Ambiance or not, it was an incredible undertaking. I think the people knew what she did for them and appreciated that hole in the wall Soup Kitchen!

In an effort to respect the dignity of the guests and make it as homelike as possible, the meals were served on glass plates, coffee and tea from real mugs, silverware and plastic table covers were on the tables for four with a small vase of flowers. Each week a volunteer would stop at a florist and retrieve his unsold flowers. Another volunteer would go out of her way to get the most elegant day old cakes from an upscale bakery. She said she had to compete with Sisters who ran a senior home for the poor who wanted the cakes for their elderly residents.

A friend of the kitchen would have a whole truck of meat delivered to us. Our people loved to have meat with a meal. A chili company would send five gallon buckets of soup to us. Though short lived, a truck of government commodities brought staples. A retired refrigerator repairman kept the critical cooling systems in order. An out of work window salesman did the handyman repairs and all at no cost to us. That didn't mean it wasn't expensive to operate and didn't require lots of fund raising to feed hundreds of hungry men, women and children five days a week.

Tuesday's regular crew were mostly ladies, lead by two intrepid, now late, friends and retired nurses. They ran the popular weekly bingo. The women would scramble through our donations and bring things they could recoup from friends and relatives. The people would crowd in the back room competing for those meager prizes like bars of soap, canned goods, a pretty bowl, a skillet, a donated set of pillowcases, a second hand hat or purse, light bulbs, a sweater, maybe paper towels and bath tissue. It wasn't unusual for the nurses to order their bridge clubs to donate swim suits in the summer and coats in the winter.

Who Came to Dinner?

The simple answer is anyone who came. There was no scrutiny or income check. Come as you are and leave when you want. People could drop by, grab a cup of coffee, stay for the meal as most did, just come and see me, or return for the afternoon and play cards. Some came once a week for Bingo. Mix and match activities. At that time we would serve a hot meal to between 300 and 350 people a day for dinner. When available, we would serve an afternoon snack.

As a group, the people had endured many losses. Dreams were dashed. Considering the place and situation, they were anonymous people without resources, perhaps deinstitutionalized and disenfranchised. Many lived marginal lifestyles. For some, their lives became even more complicated with mean coping mechanisms like alcoholism and/or substance abuse which led to even more of a downward spiral and maybe incarceration. By the time they came to us, they usually were in a profound state of loss and numb hopelessness.

Guests did not need to be homeless to come to the Kitchen. Though there were scant alternatives for them. We did have "regulars" who were disabled and elderly, but also we had people who were down on their luck due to job loss, injury or illness and transient workers who were hungry. Mostly, we didn't serve the same people every day. For the people who were lucky enough to have jobs, generally, low paying jobs, the kitchen was a godsend to partially replace or stretch their food budget. The clientele were no or low income. There were more diners under 40 than over.

Our guests, if I can fall back on the thousands of conversations and interviews over the years there, started life with hope and promise as do the rest of us. But there was a snare somewhere along the line diverting their upward trajectory. Usually there was more than one cause to what brought them there, like poverty, lack of/or completion of an education, every abuse imaginable, peer pressure, physical or mental illness, or imprisonment of themselves or significant people or even death of an important person. Unemployment and underemployment caused them to lose income and supports.

As you read the stories you will come to understand the presence and frequency of mental illness in some of our customers. To officially be considered to have one, there needs to be a diagnosis. For some who perhaps had personality disorders or were alienated from systems they could have shown symptoms that made a person highly suspicious that one existed.

Feelings of powerlessness and depression were pervasive. But one thing knit the group together. That was a prayerfulness and a faith that ignored the slams of what looked to us like their harsh lives.

Our guests were rich in talent with artists, musicians and craftsmen. Some, because of a mistake or loss of a job, were having trouble moving forward. But some just came to us to save a little money on food and enjoy seeing their friends. Some came to the kitchen because they liked the people who worked there. Guests often told us they came to the kitchen because of its reputation and respectful service. The people I seriously worked with did not want to be caught in their downward spiral. I wondered how some were able to get up in the morning, much less work their way out of the morass.

Of the people I knew and served, only a couple appeared to be comfortable with dependence. Most of the people did not want to be at a soup kitchen at all, eating someone else' choice and amount of food. They had to eat when and what we served and they may or may not have known that lunch was served at 10:00 am. in the morning with a substantial meal that ordinarily would be served at dinner. It was cafeteria style but no choices.

Those standing behind the serving counter could tell who was comfortable being in line to be served and who was new and was feeling awkward. I recall seeing an older woman in raincoat and scarf who was trying to make herself invisible enduring the waiting line for the meal. An older man who was wearing a duffer's outfit plainly looked out of place. People seemed to sense the difference in the new person and someone always merged from the line and shepherded them along, easing the stress and strangeness for the newcomer. It took courage to come to our hole in the wall.

People would follow a route from one meal to the next. I wondered how they could have a large heavy meal at our place and move on to the next soup kitchen a few blocks away and eat another lunch when it opened once we were closed. I came to see that it wasn't the need for nourishment, but a hunger for acceptance, of safety and a semblance of a social life. The warmth of the next soup kitchen extended the time they were not subject to the elements. Then, some of them would hang around the neighborhood until 4 pm when the third soup kitchen opened for service. Food did certainly meet their natural need but was also a panacea that could not address the bedrock of problems in their indigent lives.

As time went on, homelessness became institutionalized and organizations began attacking some of the core causes. Things have improved in ten plus years and various groups are taking coordinated steps to zero in on a very complex problem.

I found the people lived spontaneous lives and many didn't have watches. Procrastination prompts many social workers to post the sign "Lack of planning on your part does not constitute an emergency on my part."

The Kitchen in the Context of the Community . . .

There was a density to the number of service agencies in the area. Most of them hugged the central business district. That worked well then, but as more people lost their jobs, larger scale social service needs gradually worked their way into suburbia. Churches and communities took a share of the burden with food pantries and parish nurses. Social ministries popped up all over town. Non profits, schools and neighborhood organizations wakened to the encroaching problems and made change their mission.

Back then, in Over the Rhine, the thread of social services were lacking in continuity. Days or hours of service, requiring a client to show proof of identity and income, or appropriate gender put divisions and shook consistency and opportunity. There were soup kitchens, vets services, sandwich sources, a beauty salon and barber shop, even a gym. Shelters, pantries, a health clinic and van, dental office, a place to learn how to make jewelry, a shower house, another to create art and stops with coffee, donuts or sandwiches were sprinkled in the most populated area. One shelter was for male workers, another for women who had sons under twelve, another accepted men if they agreed to pray at a certain time and wear pajamas to bed, and one that put men into a commitment of a 12 step program. For women who were seeking employment, there was a place to get professional clothing for interviews and hopefully for actual work.

These sound like and are a lot of services but still most of the clients didn't want to be beggars. One agency would give out coupons for haircuts no sooner than six weeks apart. Then a visit to the office would have to be made to reapply and pick up the certificate before ever going to the barbershop. Many times, getting even small assistance carries with it bureaucratic red tape and time, distance, parking and energy beyond what ordinary people experience for the same matter.

The biggest shelter spilled their customers out of the warm building at 7 am in the morning. Where does one go on any day at that time? Our facility didn't open until 9:30 am so picture the misery of standing in the cold, white, or wet weather for more than a couple hours. There were no bathrooms available in that interim.

If the Kitchen received a super abundance of something, we would share it with other kitchens. When we had too many clothing donations we would tote them down to the Free Store.

Away from the soup kitchen neighborhood, there are still others who are new to the lost job, lost home ordeal and are privately trying to attack the problem. In 2008 the average income of working poor people was $9,151 which was down 2.26% from the year before. It was in this time that forclosures increased 21.2%. At the peak of the crisis 2,824,674 American people lost their homes.

This is not meant to be a criticism on prior or existing systems who all were and are sincerely trying to put a dent in an escalating problem. But at the time I worked there in the 90's, a discrepancy between what was still needed and what was provided left over 300 persons a day seeking a no cost meal, and about 10 to 15% of those customers per day seeking social services.

What's Good for the Goose is Good for the Gander!

I came to be on the receiving end and learned how some people react regarding soup kitchens and their customers. So many times I was asked why on earth I worked at "such a place" and some colleagues in my own profession took a scant view of work done there. Never spoken outright, the message rang clear that the work we did with homeless and indigent people in no way could stack up against that of elite social workers who did counseling or worked in hospitals. "I would rather work with people who got better," one told me, implying that our customers were hopeless and helpless and would stay that way. "Oh, gross!" one declared. "They give me the creeps! I'd be with a shrink all the time working with THEM!"

I didn't see my work in that light. I believed working with people who endured unforgiving situations and trying to help them gain as much control over their difficulties has a value and can make a difference. I got to see people in different scenarios, too, in my office, in the line, in the dining room, in the "back room" getting along in a recreational card or domino game or at the bingo. Once in awhile I saw the client in their home when they had one.

No doubt about it, coming to a soup kitchen can be a humbling experience for everybody and there has to be a compelling reason why the people choose to come. I never saw anyone march in with the attitude, "Oh, let's do a soup kitchen today, Dude. It's a free lunch!" I'd wager if our people had the discretionary funds, in a minute they would go to *Bob Evan's* for lunch. That is the wholesome thing to do, choose the restaurant over the soup kitchen. There is a different kind of equality among the customers there and it is tagged with a normalcy that doesn't exist with going to a soup kitchen. And that goes for the workers, too.

Really, What Do Social Workers Do?

Life at the soup kitchen was gritty. I started there managing the kitchen with a good partner. When I initiated the social services project, the cross training as manager was not expected to be lost. It showed itself with scrubbing the steam table or making mashed potatoes in the spaces between office time. It depended if I had my apron on whether or not I was in the social worker mode. I worked there while finishing school and earning my social work license. Once in the heat of the project, it was hard to leave. When I finally left there I had a Masters Degree in Social Work and a doctorate in life.

When I started the social services program, I began to wear jeans and top, as there was a theory that the service provider should not dress above the client. The clients made it known to me that they wanted me to dress like the professional I was. Early on, one gentleman sat in my office, looked around and beyond me and asked slyly, "Where is the social worker? We don't want you to dress like us!" I didn't wear suits and high heels but did accommodate them by wearing business casual outfits. Actually, that would have been my choice in the first place. Appointments were not required. People would sign up and patiently wait their turn.

Monthly, the non profit gave me a small budget with which I could purchase services for our customers. That might be a pair of work shoes or a birth certificate. Most of the clients were openly appreciative of any small help we provided. It was those little things that gave them a jump start on regaining their independence. The goal of our program, of course, was to help people help themselves.

Not all the people who came to me left with something tangible, but I did try to end on an upbeat, giving them hope and tools to begin addressing their situation. Many more were helped with emotional support, counseling, information and/or referral, contacts and resources for a solution to their problem than those who received some sort of in kind or financial assistance. I'd do my best to only refer them to a viable resource.

The people had so many barriers to just getting prepared to merge back into the mainstream. Most of us don't think twice about having a drivers' license, picture ID or birth certificate. That was one of the most frequent requests. But one can't get work without one. Can't travel without one. And can't get a prescription or cash a check without one. Most of the people could not afford a bank account. Post office boxes cost money though an option for people without an address. So they started out in a Catch 22 because they had no money to purchase one and pan handling to collect the ten to fifteen dollars to get one was discouraged. In our town, it was easier to obtain a hot meal or a snack than come by cash because begging was controlled by tight legislation in the last few years. (In 2006 Cincinnati was called one of the country's meanest cities because of unfavorable legislation effecting homeless people.)

The men told me their original document was lost in a police arrest, stolen while in the shower at the shelter, or thrown out in a sheriff's eviction action. When all your possessions are stuffed into a giant plastic bag and schlepped with you wherever you go, that sliver of paper documenting a significant component in your life might not get the same attention and care that it should. This, though the first step to getting back on one's feet, is only one of many hurdles on the way back to independence. I only gave one per person.

Some clients were good at self-advocacy, some had to learn. Okay, and here and there were a few manipulative individuals but to their surprise, their efforts were usually transparent. Depending on what they were trying to weasel out of us, I skirted their requests, but if it was serious, I'd confront them.

It would depend on what the person wanted or needed what I would help them with. We would choose the most critical goal. Maybe it was helping men get into a rehab program. Setting up a billing arrangement with a local merchant for purchase of summer fans or other commodities. I'd work with the Department of Jobs and Family Services on behalf of getting a homeless mother with kids into an apartment. I'd talk to local landlords for an elderly woman who didn't expect herself to be evicted when she didn't pay the rent. Set up a budget to make a meager check stretch the month. Climbing over somebody's burnt bridges was especially difficult. I'd meet with the teacher of a child with behavior and learning problems. Have a one on one discussion with a staff who didn't behave appropriately. Social workers in the trenches are used to multi-tasking. The following stories detail other challenges.

I had a tiny, windowless office that was once a store room. It was paneled and carpeted. Without an inch to spare, it had a desk and three chairs. One for me and two for clients. The bookshelves were opposite where clients sat and were decorated with things they enjoyed looking at. The favorite was a stack of folded quilted pillow shams. So many, especially men, commented how the the cases reminded them of their grandmothers. Add one and a half locked file cabinets and a sweet little round table with a crocheted cloth under which were stored needed items. I tried to make the room an oasis. My computer, phone, copier/fax machine were the tools of my trade. I loved that room, and was so grateful that the board saw fit to expand the soup kitchen to unusual and expensive programming.

The finite resources against the extreme need and demand of our constituents made it necessary to collaborate as much as we could with other agencies. Running our programs were the priority while making and maintaining linkages to community organizations. Working in that intense physical and emotional environment for six months without a day off was my introduction to life there. Tucked into my job was grant writing for and running summer programs for the children and arranging for informational programs like budget management and nutrition for the adults and breast health for the women.

For a couple of years, along with several other agencies in the area, we got funds from companies, foundations, organizations and churches for a Women's Day Out complete with instructional segments, entertainment, child care, and an elegant lunch. In the summer and fall we would hire a bus and take the grown ups to the woods, a place they really enjoyed because there were no trees or quiet in our part of town. Frequently, they just wanted to lie under a tree and be still. One Christmas we bussed a group to a park for it's light display then brought them back for sandwiches, cookies and hot chocolate. Pre schoolers were taken to a petting farm. We'd take families on hayrides, adults to plays, gardening, fishing and ecology activities at a local college.

When I first went to the kitchen I put together a newsletter for the staff. I didn't do that very long after I discovered it frustrated those who had low reading ability. Add on doing reports, surveys, assessment of need, outreach and speaking to groups. I had a full plate but I loved the variety and opportunity to help clients confront unique problems.

Major holidays were hard to prepare for and harder to manage. As time went on the manager and I took turns being off. One Christmas that I remember I had 360 customers, 62 volunteers who showed up eager to work and a staff of ten who had already celebrated. Though we had regular volunteers, other people begged to help on those special days and even when we would tell them we were at capacity, they would show up anyway. Without informing us women would prepare and deliver whole meals and want to contribute them to a family. We had the overstock of holiday volunteers in the office cutting cakes, in the prep room slicing meat, some chopping carrots, and onions, and peeling potatoes. People wanted to participate and give generously during the holidays. We had them playing the piano, cleaning the storerooms and visiting with guests. A father and his son came after the people were gone and scrubbed and waxed the extensive floors. Once things were done and back in order, I'd go home and prepare my own festive dinner for our family.

The Impact of Working With A Needy Group . . .

Working with people who had such intense needs resulted in heavy duty emotional and physical drain on the workers. As a social worker, I was invited to be a confidant to peoples' homelessness, abuse, unemployment, loneliness, fear and every other misery on the human spectrum. For me to be entrusted with their issues and to be a partner with them in their recovery was a privilege. Add to that the equal opportunity job description of physical work, like lifting those heavy tubs of scalding food from the oven to the hot table nibbled away at me. The discrepancy between the resources and the range of need laid heavy. The job took a lot of patience. People needed to learn basic skills that I couldn't assume were there. Money management, maturity, work hardening, there were times when I felt like once again I was starting over.

Still, I saw my role as giving my clients hope and belief in the possibility that things could change for them. In spite of their being smacked down hard so many times, I tried to help them believe they needed to be that change.

There was a spiritual tenor to our work. I did believe in the mission and what I was doing. The people reflected back to us that they appreciated our trying to treat them in a respectful, Christian manner. I ought to say that I worked hard to do that, but sometimes I'd have to go sweep the stock room, rearrange can goods or shove boxes and talk to myself to get back together. It wasn't always sweetness and light. In spite of the toll it took, the soup kitchen was dear to me. To borrow a phrase used by a priest on hearing nun's confessions, the constant pelting with requests from an insignificant personal item to an offer of marriage, was "like getting stoned to death with popcorn."

The Proof Of The Pudding . . .

Soup kitchens are intended to meet a need for nourishment and relief. Ours had more complex services. Getting a measure of change or results was difficult. I remember telling a fellow who had a prison record and who felt hopeless because he could get only marginal and temporary jobs that he might think about starting his own business. That was an angle he had never dreamed possible. I remember the surprised look on his face that morning. The fellow was miserable with his nomadic lifestyle. He said the idea was like seeing light through a crack in the door and a slice of sunshine. From there we began looking at his talents and experience and what he liked and was good at doing. There were new programs, job incubators that might hold possibility for him. With the biggest impediment his having a police record, he was not alone.

The Cincinnati Enquirer recently reported that Ohio lawmakers are working on legislation that will remove some of the barriers confronted by one in six Ohioans who are non-violent offenders. They would be able to work in certain industries and to get a driver's license. Those effected by the removal of the restrictions could merge into the work force reducing the rate of recidivism.

My clients were clever, quick minded, creative. Why couldn't they use their talents on their own behalf? Sometimes this suggestion rang home. One young woman started her own cleaning company, a man opened a catering service. Some of our ladies went to a women's center and learned how to design and make earrings and other jewelry. They were justifiably proud to have a new skill and a way to subsidize their income. Single mom's went to school or work and learned how to juggle child care, transportation and schedules. They needed support during that transition. Men came to have a new respect for their bodies and nurtured their health and souls at a religious men's gym.

My efforts were to work on an individual and systemic level to improve the situation or make a change. Progress was and still is too slow for sure. The precise measure of my work was unknown to me because of the transitory population. Not everybody I worked with had a goal to end their homelessness. I could work intensely with a person, then, they would not return and not having an address, follow-up was not possible.

Homelessness wasn't and still is not limited to people who live outside the boundaries of accepted society. It can happen to anyone and I have seen this often. None of us is exempt from a catastrophic illness, an accident or injury, or extended unemployment after a well paying job. It's impact can result in loss of a home and instability with long reaching effects. I am not asking for pity for these people, just to look at them with sensitivity and try not to make judgments.

Homelessness is dangerous to a person's health. Most probably the exhausted homeless person you see loping along, pushing a burdened grocery cart or toting grocery bags with their only belongings, is coping with some sort of unaddressed condition or disease.

A 2010 study by the University of Cincinnati Institute for Policy Research showed black adults were more likely than their white peers to have potentially serious health conditions, have inappropriate medical care, have old unpaid medical bills. The Center for Disease control reports that death rates for black Americans surpass those of Americans overall for heart disease, cancer, diabetes, HIV and homicide. The disproportionately high numbers of homeless African Americans fall easily into these statistics.

One could not work or volunteer at the Kitchen without being effected by whom we were serving and what we were trying to do. We knew we were working with a fragile, vulnerable group. One consolation was that for most people, homelessness is not a permanent living arrangement. Readings indicate that usually it is a crisis situation and doesn't last longer than a couple awful years. Our contribution to that bitter time was that we tried to make the moments they were in our Kitchen as beneficial as possible.

Gradually as the economy changed and downgraded, more Caucasian people joined the lines but always a slow second to their confrères.

For most people homelessness is not a permanent living arrangement. Readings indicate that usually it is a crisis situation and doesn't last longer than a couple awful years. Though, in one place, I read a chronically homeless person lived like that for 40 years. The longer a person is homeless the more they become isolated even from their peers. Their condition becomes very complex and entrenched and is very likely to be confounded by alcohol or substance abuse and/or mental illness.

Why people become evicted

WHY PEOPLE BECAME EVICTED AND HOMELESS

One month, I tallied why people said they were losing their apartment, were at risk of eviction, or were already without a place to live. It follows that without a fairy godmother, homelessness is not far behind.

The reasons told to me were . . .

- she had lived with someone else who died. His kids came and took everything in the apartment but her personal clothes.
- she was kicked out by her room mate. The person she was living with ended their relationship.
- she was beaten by her room mate.
- she no longer could be sheltered by her host because he lost his job.
- her host was being evicted because she had a person in the apartment who was not on the lease.
- he could no longer stay at his relative's house sleeping on the couch.

They themselves . . .

- lost their full time job. Part time jobs didn't pay rent.
- had gone to jail long enough to miss a rent payment.
- were in the hospital just long enough to lose their apartment and their belongings including their personal papers.
- made a mistake in how they used their money.
- thought they would win more than they lost.
- had to pay child support and there wasn't enough left to put on rent.

- had the children's pictures taken and didn't save enough for rent.
- got hurt on the job and couldn't work.
- had a stroke and still was too sick to work.
- lived in a market rate apartment and were waiting for Supplemental Security Income, Social Security or Worker's Compensation decisions.
- were kicked out because her kids broke the building rules by being too noisy.
- were evicted with everyone else in the building due to drug sales going on.
- were evicted along with her son because he did drugs. That is the law. But didn't know he was selling drugs and never did them herself.
- were evicted because the landlord said she had too much company.

Now this is just a sample. Though I know these above reasons are true and certainly possible, I also know there are honest to goodness and fair reasons why people get the boot for breaking rules and doing things that are not legal. Some clients are disinclined to tell me that part up front.

My job as a social worker was to help the clients help themselves. In the spirit of peace and justice, when all other options were explored, I helped when I could, usually with matching funds from the person's own industry or some other person or organization. I could have emptied the coffers on the first of every month had I responded to every request for support.

As custodian of the social welfare funds of the organization I needed to distribute them as judiciously as I could and stretch them through the month. People would tell such compelling stories. Sometimes they were true and sometimes not. I had no crystal globe. People would wait to ask for help until the very last minute and though I'm sure they were embarassed by their procrastination, I was not their fairy godmother and just wouldn't do a disappearing act for someone who was capable of managing their money.

Copies of eviction notices and dunning bills were required and phone calls to confirm amounts were made to landlords. I'd coax and ask for extra time for the client to get the funds. Turning the apartment over was expensive, I'd say. If this was the first time it happened, it was easier to win a few days extra to collect the rent money. And if we helped in part, I took the payment directly to the landlord, management company, shoe store, power company or pharmacist. Any decision I made requiring a check was cleared through the bookkeeper.

People just getting an apartment needed everything. We used donations of household goods from people downscaling. Families gave us clothing from someone who had died or grown out of them. Mothers who were in a shelter needed the most basic of items. If their sons left their underpants on the floor the pants were thrown out. Workers needed gloves and socks. On really frigid days, every man coming through the food line got a pair of brown work gloves. If we had an abundance of bath soap, a bar was handed out with the meal. Bigger and nicer donated items were used as prizes at the weekly bingo. A flashy belt, purse, a toaster, a sauce pan with dish soap and, glory be, a box of laundry soap were vied for. Skeptics would tell us that a bar of soap or a roll of toilet tissue could go for a quarter on the nearby market. We had no investigator to follow the client to see if what we gave them was sold on the street. We would never stalk someone suspecting they were misleading us. These were second hand items usually, and if someone worked their way through all the screening mechanisms for a pair of second hand socks or deodorant sample, so be it. My boss, an empathic woman, said they needed it more than we did.

Fortunately, I had a small petty cash fund. I used it to buy hand warmers, tooth brushes, tooth paste, combs, small things like a pair of socks, a new rubber tip for the end of a cane. I never gave cash, and when someone sat before me with new nails, expensive hair style, gold jewelry and leather coat, I was *super* cautious. Just because a person didn't manage their income appropriately did not mean we would come to the rescue.

One day a new customer, an elderly man, visited me saying he had gone to the casino and had lost his whole monthly check. He had blown his rent, food and gas money and consequently lost his apartment. He stayed at the shelter and got his car impounded because he parked it in the wrong spot. He came to the soup kitchen to eat and find out what he could do. I called his sister who lived in another town who agreed to pay the bus fare for him to get to her house. She said she would keep him 'til the next check came. This gentleman was slow cognitively, but knew well he had done something "dumb." he said. Word went around the kitchen detailing all the man's losses and how they came to be. He wasn't shy about explaining his dilemma. It was a good lesson for everyone. Many times, the problem was not resolved so easily.

In the middle of winter, I opened the door to the kitchen for the morning session. A blast of frigid air bowled me back against the brick wall. A young woman who had previously told me she "does tricks" and was known to have a drug habit stood there shivering. I asked her why she didn't have a coat. "I lost it," she stammered. "Wait here and I will get you one." We had donated coats from our volunteers. I took one to her. That was 9:30 am. At 1 pm I opened the door for the afternoon session and again she was standing there hugging her bare arms, rubbing her goose bumps.

"Fool me once, shame on you. Fool me twice, shame on me," said Abraham Lincoln.

And now—story time!

Part Two

CARLA

One day, a young woman called me before office hours.
"I am being evicted," she cried into the phone.
"When?"
"Right now.
The sheriff is hauling all my stuff out this minute."
"Didn't you know your landlord was going to court?
Didn't you know this was going to happen?
Didn't you receive notice?"
"The manager told me not to worry.
She told me she'd take care of it.
I never thought she would do this.
She was always so nice to me."
I knew that once Carla's case had been taken to court, there could be no negotiation or delay.
She was losing all her possessions.
The echo of this circumstance seemed to reverberate within the brick and cement canyons of the neighborhood.
"Eviction! Eviction! Eviction!"
"Come see me and I will help you find a place to stay," I replied.

The now homeless woman was mildly retarded and totally without support. She did not want to be a part of any system.
She wanted to take care of herself.
One more young woman starting over.
We had some work to do together.
Add one more statistic.
Blame is useless at this stage.

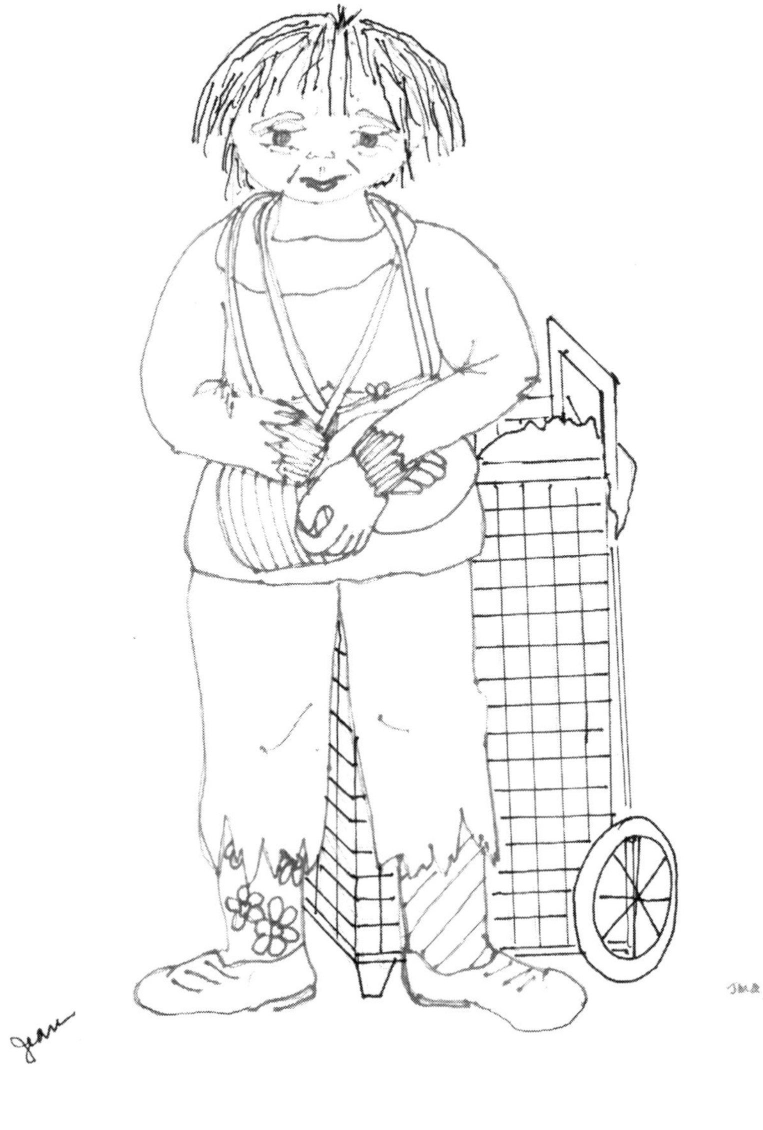

JEAN

What a typical image of a bag lady, you might say.
Jean was in her 70's.
Bewhiskered,
crotchety,
and demanding.
She schlepped a metal grocery cart behind her.
It listed under the weight of her bulging trash bags.
Almost as if to insulate herself against the pain of her homelessness,
she wore all of her clothes at once.
Today Jean got evicted—again!
In bittersweet response to the nasty task ahead of him,
her landlord called Adult Protective.
"She needs help.
But she can't stay here without paying her rent!"
AP brought her to us.
It's not the first time this happened to Jean.
I called her son, who came right over,
but she resisted his help.

Then the policeman came to take her to the hospital for a three day hold.
Her son didn't know how else to help her.
"Would you give her one last meal before they take her" he cried.
Jean yelled to me,
"Gimme some of those damn beans!"
What will become of her?

monica

MONICA

For years, she taught school.
Third grade to be exact.
A tough, exacting taskmaster, we are told.
And now, she gave report cards
to the cooks at the soup kitchen.
Each morning she sat at the same place in the dining room.
in the same outfit.
"An eccentric!" some wagged.
"She's rich!" others observed.
"I heard she owns some houses!"
"Then how come she lives out of her car?" another would chime in.
"There's barely enough room to drive!"
"She's a hoarder!"
Someone called the cops when they saw something small and dark moving in the rear car window.
She was tested at the hospital and released with the statement as
"Not a danger to herself or anyone else.
Bathing is a personal choice.
Where she sleeps isn't relevant."
Monica would howl when things didn't go her way.
A decisive woman.

Many of our customers lived on the periphery of society.
Monica fussed when her meal wasn't just right.
Her lifestyle wasn't our business unless she asked for help,
but she never did.
She was a guest for dinner.
We worried.
We did think she was a risk to herself,
and could be in danger of getting bit by a four legged raider in her car.
She would suffer from the heat or cold living in her auto.
Her bad throat needed intervention.
Yes, she, too, wasn't well.
She wouldn't deal with the cancer that was gnawing in her throat.
Taking her lead, we offered her the usual,
A cup of java, one real cream, and two pink sweet stuff.

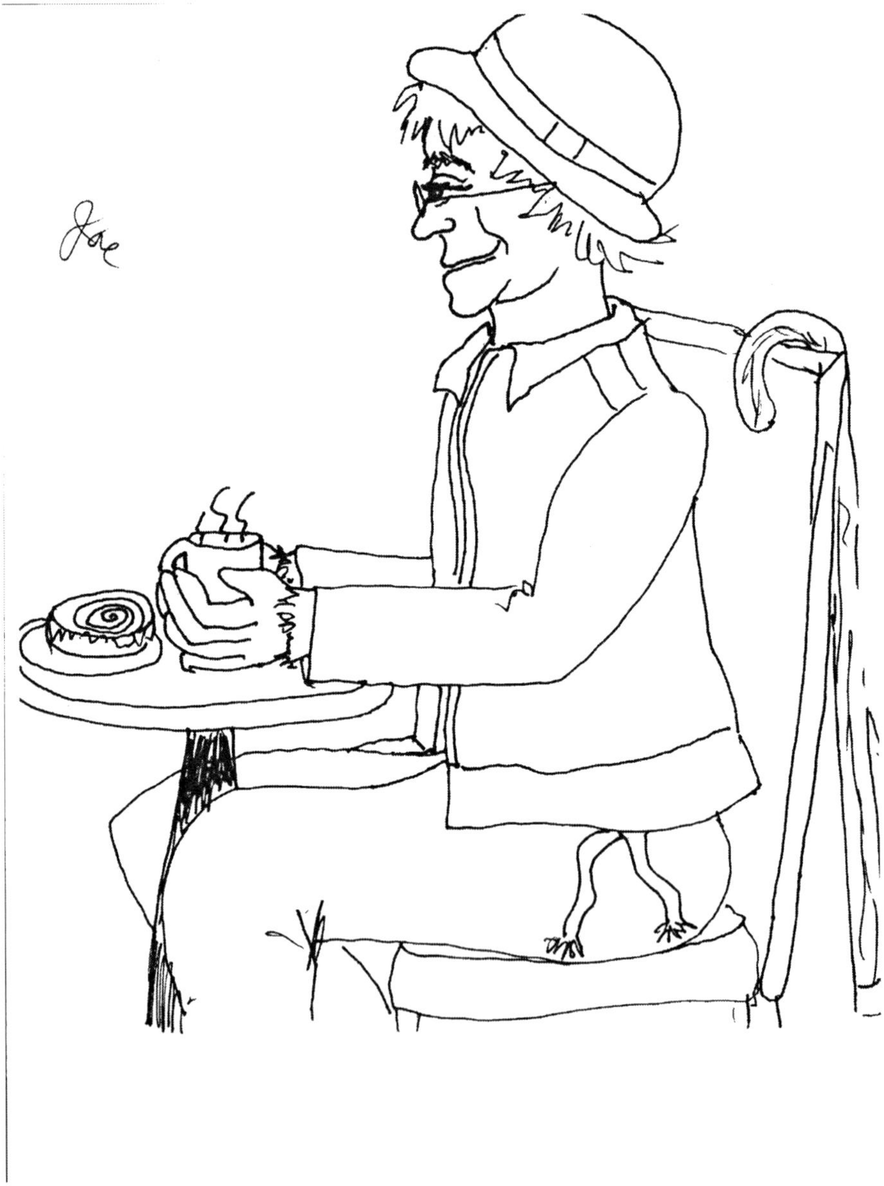
Joe

JOE

80 something, he was
such a cute old guy.
His burgundy corduroys were lassoed by shoe strings
tied together looking like rosary beads.
Each morning he supped at the soup kitchen,
the reward after his two mile walk.
You knew where to find Joe,
same time, same station.
His round, smiling face was in a perpetual wink.
sans one eye.
People said he couldn't talk.
But we knew he could work his crowd.
The workers bustled behind the counter
seasoning the day's repast.
He tapped his mug on the table and grinned.
Low and behold,
breakfast appeared before him.
One day he didn't show up.
We learned his pipes couldn't stop leaking and
he was placed in a nursing home.
That made his young wife mad because
there went his check!

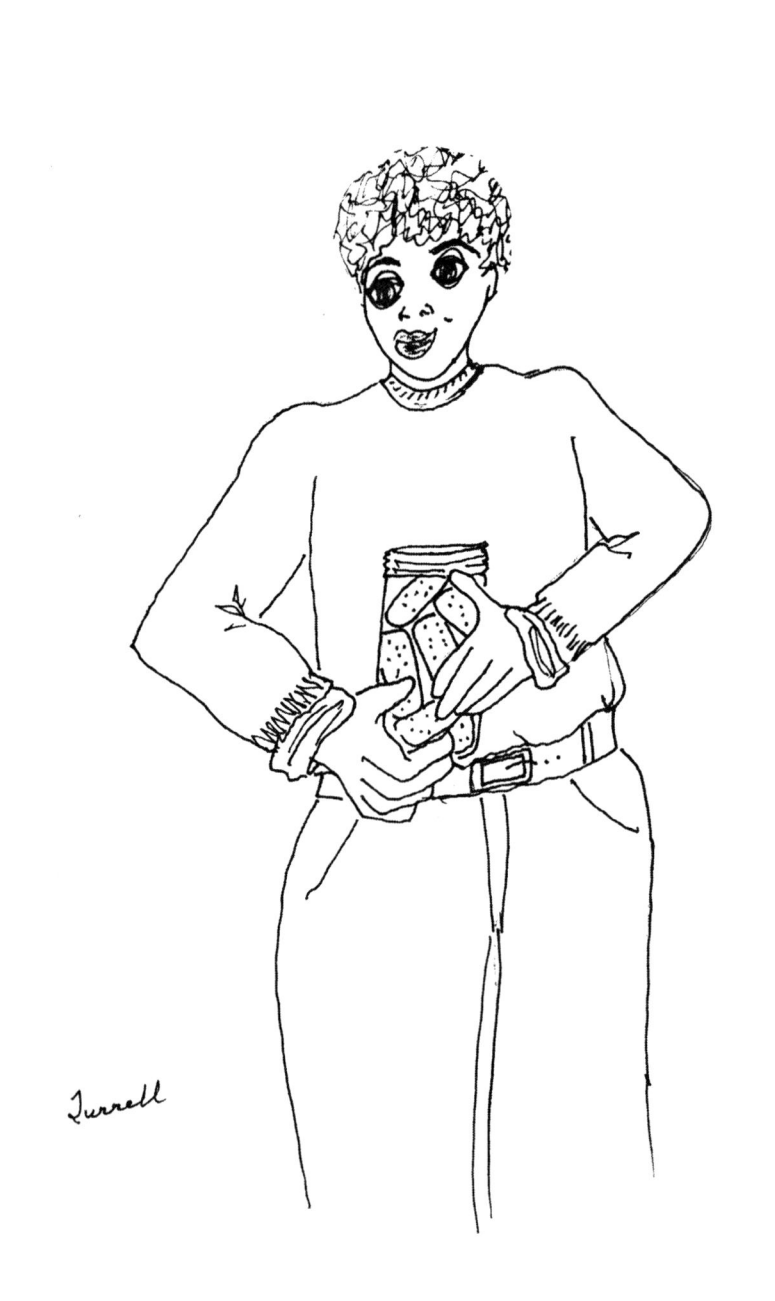

Turrell

TURRELL

Turrell stood blocking the storeroom door.
That is no trouble.
He's a HUGE guy
bustin' his seams and
overflowing his tattered work pants.
As I reached up to unlock the door,
he took my hand and said,
"I want that!"
Speaking of my 35 year old wedding ring.
"No way, Turrell, it's mine forever!"
"Well then, I'll have to take the finger with it," he blustered.
"I find no humor in this conversation," I fumed.
This is as close as I ever came to a threatening situation.
I doubt "T" was fully serious.
Generally, the people took care of us.
Like, "Here come the meter maids,
you better move your car!"
Nonetheless,
my hand shook as I dug into the sugar.

GEORGIA

Such a pretty Mom
with seven unsmiling kids.
Each had a different Dad.
Georgia's eviction was a repeat performance.
Many came to her rescue.
They said they couldn't let those babies sleep on the street that night.
To make a long story short
she was thrilled to stay at the infamous, now late, Exeter Hotel.
She would keep us up to date on her travail.
Finally, after counting 35 days, she found her dream apartment,
away, she told us, from the druggies and guns of the ghetto.
It wasn't long, though, that
we learned the kids had been taken from her.
She showed up at the kitchen door.
So drunk.
So sad.
I couldn't let her in like that.
We both knew
it wasn't food she needed.
She zig zagged down the lane.
I stood there helpless.

ANTONIO

He had a problem with women who's bread had gone to waist.
But what did it matter!
He met his wife at the old Lewis Center,
a way station for the mentally ill.
Antonio was homeless.
Whenever he wanted to come in from out of the blistering cold or icy rain
he would cut himself.
He knew the arrest would buy him a few days from the elements.
He had the scars to prove it.

IRIS

As soon as the heavy steel door opened,
we knew who was entering.
She trotted into the soup kitchen,
her fragrance preceding her.
Her wardrobe: a long black unhemmed skirt,
linty with kitty fur,
leopard boots untied.
A torn, soiled, droopy tee shirt which said,
JESUS IS A BLACK MAN.
Keys jangled from her neck.
A homemade rabbit fur coat snuggled over her shoulders.
A city official said "she's hygienically challenged."
The guests moaned when she came near.
Ice white hair sprouted from her pink scalp.
But the people cut her some slack.
We worried about Iris.
Downtown people knew her by name.
Way back, a high fever changed her
from being a suburban wife, mother and grad student.
We all knew she wasn't the daughter of a dead President and

had not had affairs with rich magnets.
Her son's father wasn't Neil Diamond.
The soup kitchen gave Iris an 80th birthday party
which she accepted graciously,
still dressed in her personally designed conversation piece.
The truth of the matter was
Iris was dying of breast cancer and
had taken better care of her pooch
which she referred to as her hearing dog.
One morning she didn't bustle into pick up her orange juice, cake and pie.
Word spread among the social service agencies to watch for her.
Iris had found her way to the hospital
where all the king's doctors and nurses boo hoo'd.
They couldn't fix Iris's one where there used to be two.

ALLEN

"My nemesis," I used to call him.
Of all the guests we served,
Allen demanded the most from me.
Inside.
Whatever his diagnosis,
he marched to his own drummer.
He was cantankerous to the last word.
"Sometime I'm going to Anchorage!"
he promised.
"That's nice!" we'd counter!
Picture this:
The laundry was calling him.
So was the bath.
The folks took the long way around him.
He wouldn't go to the shower house because
twenty minutes under water was too short, he said.
Allen was a little fellow.
Toothless.
He wanted to touch everything.
No one wanted to wash his thermos.
He would order a special lunch.
One day, he called and said,

"Guess where I am?"
"The El Durado?"
His favorite motel.
He would go there for the first couple of days of the month.
"No, I'm in Kansas!"
Dorothy would be so pleased I said to myself!
(Oh, shame on me!)
"I'm on my way to Anchorage!" he bragged!
So Allen fulfilled his dream and did not return as long as I was there.
I am embarrassed to admit this, but
whoever helps Allen in the 49th state,
bless your heart!

MITCHELL

The first time I saw Mitchell,
I was so sad.
He was a tall, handsome, intelligent looking man.
But you had to look beyond his dirty, gnarled fingers,
his bare feet and his high water pants.
And hold your breath.
He'd hide his spirits in his coffee mug.
And growl at us when we wouldn't let him sleep on the freezer.
But Mitchell is gone now.
He won't bother the church goers for a quarter.
He won't fuss for a vegetarian meal.
He won't fall off the loading dock.
A twelve step program won't help him either.
But maybe now,
Relieved of his torments,
He could give us a hand with some of his buddies.

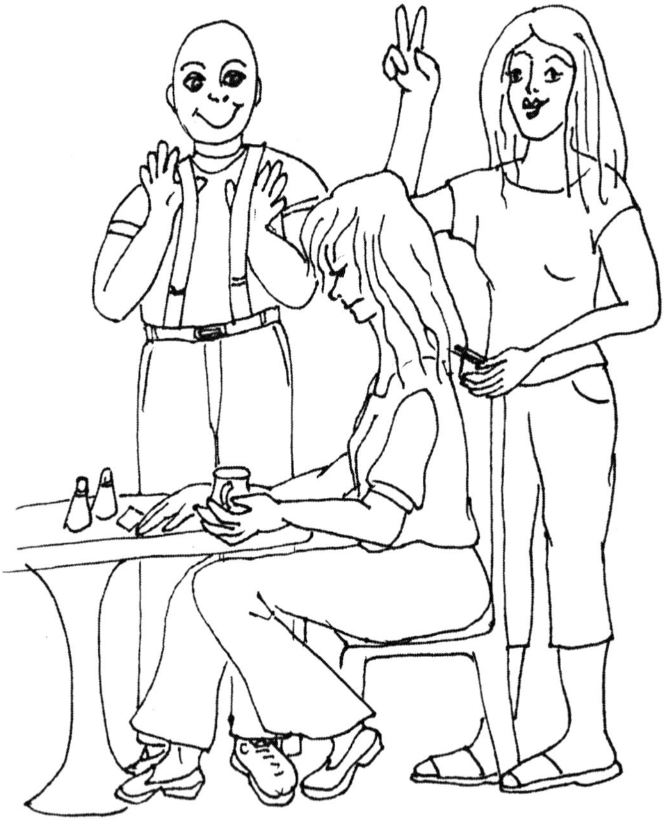

Baby mama

BABY MAMA

A disturbance interrupted the mid day meal.
Back slapping and congratulations centered on one young fellow
because he announced
his pending fatherhood.
Following shortly was a young woman who looked peaked and nauseous.
She only wanted tea and crackers that day.
And she wasn't strutting proudly as she gripped the table edge
to keep from swooning to the floor.
Her Mom was bragging to her lunch partners
that grandparenthood was about to be hers.
A month later I had long forgotten the drama.
It was Baby Mama's Mother's turn to be pale and gripping the dinner table.
I felt out of sync with the scene before me.
"Middle class judgmental bitch!" I chided myself.
This is no fairy tale.
The worst part of the story is that at the other end of these pregnancies, two infants were taken from their mothers (and fathers)
by the powers that be.

And life at the soup kitchen went on undisturbed.
Except for me—
I was plenty upset at the incongruity of their situations
and wished for those babies it had never happened.
I watched the mother, daughter and father for clues to how they felt
after such an awful upheaval and loss,
but none were there to be seen.
I observed that many of the young women who came through the kitchen did not have children with them.
It was a day of celebration when one of them
did bring her newborn for us to enjoy.
For some time I meditated on these cultural differences
and struggled mightily to make some sense out of it.
I was a xeno, a stranger, trying to understand what I had just experienced,
but could only be close enough to be a voyeur.

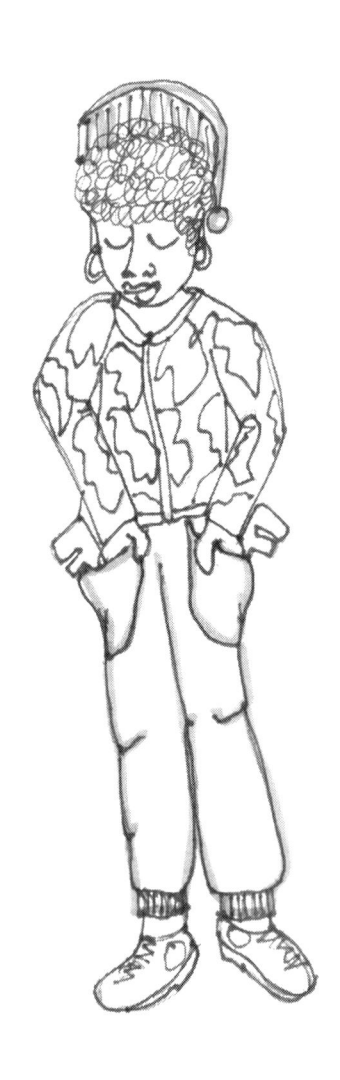

KENNETH

Kenny stood against the shiny kitchen wall
with hands deep in his army fatigue jacket.
A fuchsia knitted cap drooped over his ears.
A rusty wrench sagged in each of his pants pockets.
"They would protect us," he smiled.
His chartreuse sweat pants bagged at the knees.
Kenny's history at one point would never have predicted
this sad state of affairs.
The kitchen historians believed he once owned a home,
had some kids, and
even had a business.
At one point he owned a car.
Kenny couldn't tell me.
They all agreed that somebody slipped Kenny a
powerful Mickey Finn one night.
He's never been the same.
Kenneth lived in an unheated, unlighted set of rooms
he told me.
He collected canned goods and
they were "lined up for miles," a neighbor added.
"How do you manage to stay there in the winter?" I
asked concerned.
"No problem, I high jack the electricity with an
extension cord.

My neighbor says it's OK."
His neighbor was his girlfriend.
"If it is cold, I use a heater."
Kenny owed a zillion to the power company he told me one day.
Do you have water? Thinking of the sanitation aspect of his shelter.
Guessing he lived in an abandoned building,
because he would have been evicted without electricity,
I didn't want to push his trust in me and
risk his losing the one place that was safe for him.
He gets A for resourcefulness.
As long as Kenneth took his medicine, he was functional in a limited way.
If he ran out of or forgot to take the meds,
he would de-compensate and
need to be taken to the hospital.
We watched Kenny closely given how he was acting.
We just said him that morning,
"Check your wrenches here!"
He grinned, curtsied and willingly relinquished his weapons.

BIG BOY

You never knew whether he was putting you on
or telling the honest to God truth.
He was nicknamed Big Boy
and he had a story for everything.
He was the personality of the kitchen.
Add to that, the bouncer,
the baker,
the mechanic,
and only he knew how to fix the stove.
He told me he fathered fifteen kids and
he had had his own business in the suburbs before his
life slid down hill.
One of his sons came to the kitchen and confirmed
some of the
historical aspects in the life of our star employee.
Big would tell the most outrageous tales.
And he loved women!
One day he whispered to a lady guest,
(With tongue in cheek, I hope!)
"Tammy, my dear, it's time to start our family!"
All the while, rubbing his Buddha tummy.

He didn't do that again!
Big would, we knew, drink merrily after leaving work.
One day, his wife called telling us he had a fatal heart attack
On the way to his job.
We miss Big Boy still.
So do the bill collectors.
They sounded *real* sad when they called and we told them
he was no longer with us!

GENEVIEVE

Genevieve lived her whole life in Over the Rhine.
She celebrated her 84th birthday in the nursing home.
Her husband and family crowded around her,
two sons and two daughters.
A couple more awaited her in heaven.
She was restless that day
and tried to climb over the bars of her bed.
That wasn't a good idea.
So her husband of well more than 60 years
tried diverting her attention.
"No," demanded she,
"I want to go across the hall!"
"Hon," he cautioned,
"It is too far to walk and besides,
it's just an old stock room."
Attention diverted, her fingers knotted around the bars.
Then they traced the hem of her pastel afghan.
For a moment, she seemed to be pondering
something deep and wonderful.
She called her husband to her.

His tallness crinkled down to her pale face on the pillow.
"Well then," she whispered,
"Let's make love!"
With a history of many magic moments between them,
he blushed and smiled a memory wrapped smile!
"Later, sweety!"

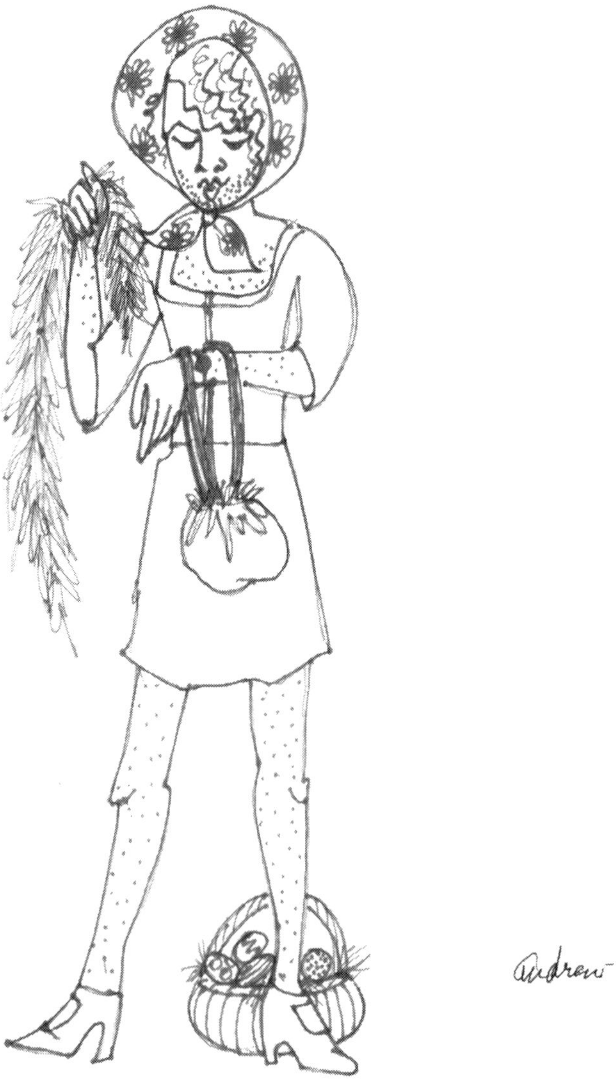

ANDREW

Andrew enjoyed exchanging his plain man clothes for high heels and
gold lame'.
One Holy Week, a donor provided 350 filled Easter baskets for the
soup kitchen customers.
The local newspaper caught wind of such generosity and
sent a photographer to freeze frame our guests' moment of delight.
Andrew groomed himself in his pascal finery.
So busy with his toilet, he forgot to shave his legs.
He begged the newsman to snap him in his rosy boa and
blond wig, and to catch him balancing on his pointy toed stilts.
But the photographer reneged.
Taking Andrew's picture like this would be invasive.
It would be embarrassing to Andrew and others, he believed.
Andrew insisted and pleaded for a photo that would capture him
sporting his skirt and open necked blouse.
The sea of lunch guests parted for him to seat himself against

the brick wall, under the black wall phone.
He smoothed his pleats 'til they suited him,
then finally crossed his legs and
announced that he felt pretty.
The reluctant photographer confided to me
that the picture would NEVER be published.
He said he would send the print straight to our elite
customer.
Andrew grinned proudly.
The gold caps on his teeth glistened in the flash's
reflected light.
Our star skipped lunch that day.
It seemed his peers wanted nothing to do with his
escapade and
goaded him until he left.
The bunny baskets made the paper with all good
dignity.
As promised, I never saw the donation to Andrew's
portfolio.
When he returned, he was wearing his civies, and
never mentioned it again.

HEFTY MAN

Bald as a cue ball.
A BIG, stunning Afro man,
as gentle as a puppy.
Size alone told you not to mess with him.
A keeper of the peace in the most literal sense,
he was trained and worked as a security guard.
His demeanor was always respectful and professional.
One day lunch needed to be taken to a very sick man
who lived on one of the meanest streets in the city
on the second floor way back between two buildings.
We didn't ordinarily deliver lunches in the neighborhood.
But I was asked to do it as a favor by an inner city home nurse.
On the best day,
it was not a safe thing to do.
Even Hefty Man was cautious to go there.
"If two of us go together we'll be fine," I observed,
(Maybe because I am too dumb and naïve to say no.)
I added to myself that
maybe I should take a hint from the volunteers
who walked lunch to nearby senior residents.
The volunteers always declined requests to deliver on that mean street.

As we walked over cracked pavements and
passed booze bottles peeking from crumpled brown bags,
he asked me why I had asked him to accompany me.
"You are a good guy,
I've known you a long time and I feel safe with you."
He was blown away, as they say.
Having somebody believe in him was a rare feeling.
We found our way to a court yard surrounded on four sides.
Our whispers held a hallow sounding echo.
We had to call up to the man who then rung us in to a dim stairwell.
He was back on the couch when we got upstairs.
We found him too sick to eat.

Cheri

CHERI

Cheri was taken home to her room by the police,
Over and over and over.
"An unruly," they'd say in cop talk.
"A drinking problem" to put it mildly.
At her worst, she'd find her way to her friend
In the soup kitchen,
And go into the DT's!
Whooping! Catching butterflies!
In her own orbit.
The rules would not allow her to stay in that condition.
But that doesn't happen any more.
Cheri was being treated for lung cancer.
The xrays burned her throat and chest.
She was too thin.
Her once attractive face was puffed and distorted.
She didn't complain.
Not one word!
Sadly, she still smoked,
Exacerbating, what she said was just a bad cold.
Maybe trying to put a haze on remembering the sad life behind her.

Abuse. Rape. Poverty. Loneliness. Alcoholism. Mental illness.
She always wore a crusty cover to her behavior.
Underneath her tough facade was a fragile little girl.
In pain.
Family and friends had faded away
As had any wholesome, sweet memories.
I always imagined her as once a business woman,
Fully competent, running the shop.
I think I'll stick with that.

LORENZO

Tall, pleasant and balding,
Lorenzo liked to talk about his parents
who were Italian and African American.
"It makes for interesting menus," he would chuckle.
Lorenzo was going on sixty.
He couldn't work anymore as a bus driver
because of terrible headaches.
When he wasn't feeling badly,
he would keep the people around him in stitches.
Lorenzo said ordinarily he wouldn't come to the kitchen
but he didn't have enough cash to see him through the month.
"I know it sounds silly," he confided,
"I am still paying child support.
My ex wife took me to court
saying I didn't pay what I was supposed to.
She lied, right there to the judge.
The truth was,

I paid her faithfully,
but I did it in cash.
I had no receipts,
no canceled checks or
money order slips to prove it.
So here I am,
an old man,
Paying for my kids who are all over 18.
How mean can a person get?"
he asked somberly.

Part Three

Jamar

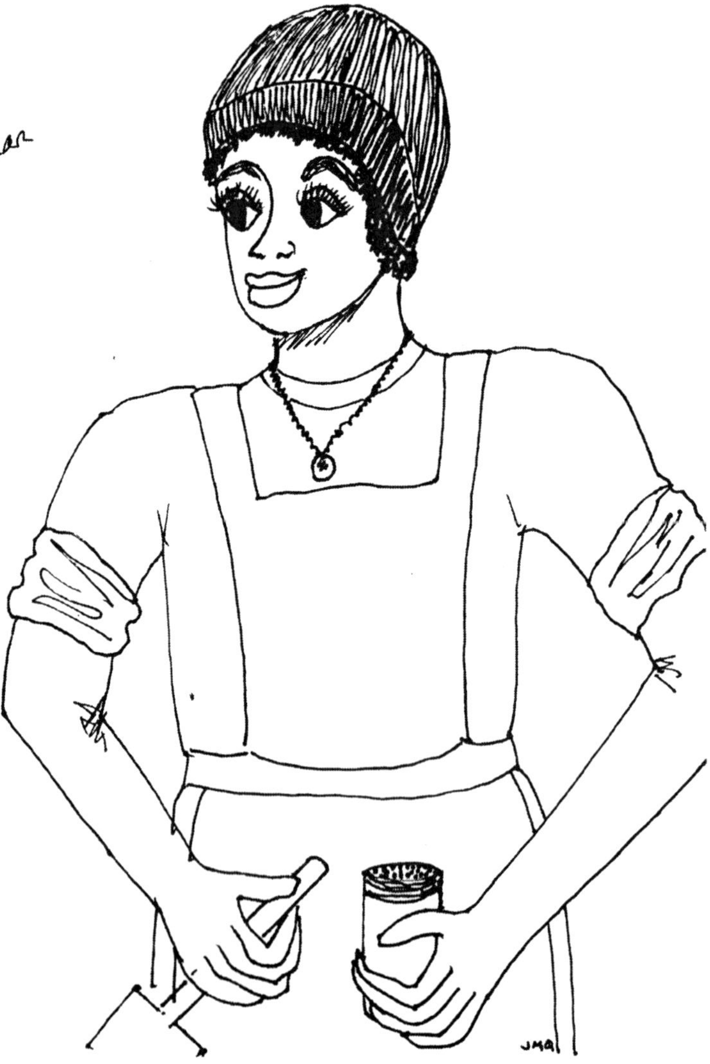

"IF YOU LIE, YOU STEAL"

Mom

**For awhile he seduced
some with his clever crack act.
He paid the piper.**

Jamar Davis

It was seven in the morning and 32 year old Jamar sat in my office drenched in sweat. He blurted out that he was in trouble. He "was sick again," he whispered. The night before he had spent $100 on crack cocaine. He bought the drugs by selling a comforter set and household items.

I had known Jamar for over four years. He was an engaging fellow who had had an awful childhood with gross physical and emotional abuse. Both parents died from complications of substance abuse when he was in grade school leaving him to be raised *laissez faire* by relatives and friends. In his early twenties, he was shot in the head, resulting in a permanent metal plate placed in his skull. Like other addicts, he lied so convincingly, or thought he did, that he clouded dark issues about himself, severely risking his life.

For two years, he was in a residential recovery program which was housed in a sad tattered mansion in a nearby neighborhood. While there, he was diagnosed as psychotic schizophrenic and was placed on medication. Those symptoms were evident when he was decompensated due to illegal drug use.

Seven months ago, he completed the program and reluctantly had to leave. After living at a men's transitional living program, he moved to a bare three room fourth floor apartment in the heart of a drug area. I recalled trying to convince him to get a place in a neighborhood away from his buddies where he wouldn't be as easily tempted to fall back into his old ways. He said he was confident in his ability to withstand the temptations around him. Besides, he confessed, he couldn't afford anything else on what was left of his social security check after he paid child support for four of his seven children.

While Jamar was in recovery he was a cheerful, excellent cleaner and strong volunteer. I learned that two months ago he slacked off in attending his support meetings. It was a no brainer when he admitted he returned to smoking pot with his girl friend and succumbed to old druggie friends' peer pressure.

Just a couple of weeks before, I had arranged and had taken him to the substance abuse center for what he said was pot and alcohol. He was in treatment for a week. The staff there discharged him, after extending his treatment by four days because they believed "he had potential." I knew Jamar had been addicted to alcohol, but had no clue he was back using crack cocaine. I don't know how he took his drug, i.e., orally, inhaled, injected or smoked it. The effects last briefly about 30 minutes. Afterward, withdrawal can include extreme fatigue, depression and suicidal urges. The user can be paranoid, anxious, grandiose and hyper sexual. They can have a high fever and even seizures.

Jamar's engaging personality and persuasive style of communicating even seduced his doctors. A few days before, he was having heart pains and went to the emergency room. Some of the side effects of that drug are increased blood pressure and even a fatal heart attack. Initially, he charmed his doctors, delaying a diagnosis of his crack addiction. He didn't have the look of a down and out addict. He was well groomed with shiny teeth, a hair cut and clean, pressed clothes. It must have taken enormous strength to hide his addictions.

He only had a mattress on the floor of his tidy apartment and a tiny TV. The rest of his furniture must have been sold. He admitted he stole to support his relapse, some of it coming from the soup kitchen. Odd things sell on the street, cups, silverware, someone's hat, a bunch of carrots. He was quick and clever at hiding his booty until it was time to leave.

Anything that could be was locked down at the kitchen was, but people still found ways to snatch things that weren't nailed down. Even a slice of cake waiting to be served at the meal, a spice or a stirring spoon could disappear.

Such a pleasant young man was bearing the burdens of natures' limitations, severe loss, a twisted rearing and temptations of a sick neighborhood. Another time I drove him to the rehab program, hoping this time it would work permanently. Frankly, I told him that we have finite bodies and they become irreparably damaged by continued use of cocaine. Alcohol and other substances erode our organs and fry our brain cells. I hated to see him harm himself. He wasn't fooling anyone but himself by pretending he was clean. I told him I wished better for him. He cried all the way to the facility. I told him this was the last time I was going to be a part of his addiction.

The destination was a shabby building on a busy thoroughfare and he probably couldn't hear me wish him good luck and good health. Jamar grabbed his small tote stuffed with a few clothes and personal items. He would be searched before he settled in. He trotted up the steps, not looking back. I held my breath that he wouldn't come running back out once he saw me leave the premises. The door stayed closed and I could see the director greeting him.

Franklin Thomas

"I LEARNED TO NOT WRITE MY NAME ON THE WALL!"

With barriers as high as Everest. He forged his dream and won!

FRANKLIN THOMAS

This is a story of Franklin Thomas, reflecting back to 1994 when he was a soup kitchen volunteer. Sometimes we needed extra assistance beyond what paid staff could handle. For the people of the community, volunteering or working at the kitchen was seen as an honor. We would have helpers from elegant neighborhoods on the service line next to homeless people and it worked just fine. The people who were consumers of our services were hired often and were dedicated workers. Though not a formal program, it was intended to enhance their work skills and give them experience that could be used to get another job.

For homeless people, volunteering could get them out of the weather from 7 am on. Thirty four year old, six foot Franklin, a muscular African American man, was one of those helpers. He was proud of his physique and loved his black curly hair. However, he was embarrassed about being homeless. He said he lived in College Hill, a suburb of Cincinnati. His splattered painter's cap was worn backwards, and day after day he had on the same overalls and shirt.

There was a lot of rehabbing going on in the neighborhood and he had been lucky enough to be hired as a house painter several times. But there was a lull in available jobs and he came to the soup kitchen to fill in his time and get out of the weather after being discharged from the homeless shelter. He was knowledgeable about jazz music and was a drummer by avocation.

Cooperative and energetic, Franklin would tote cases of vegetables and other supplies from the storeroom. He would open those cans with the industrial size can opener in blitz time. We came to realize he might not be able to read well when he would consistently bring beans instead of peas. At first we thought he wasn't paying close attention but this happened repeatedly. No job was too mean and he did his tasks quickly and well.

Franklin was born in a tiny town in northern Tennessee. His father had been an airplane pilot and was then an insurance investigator and his mother worked two jobs as a nurse. His parents were married when he was born. He believed they were alcohol dependent. His mother, he confided, was his nemesis, having had too many boyfriends. His sister is a teacher who is ten years younger than he. His parents divorced when he was very young due to his father abusing his mother. Franklin said he has four half brothers and two half sisters by his parents' second marriages. He called himself just a country boy, adding that there was a lot of "fightin' and arguin'" when he was at home. He was physically punished many times and could go into gruesome and graphic detail of particular beatings.

His mother moved to the big city while he was in grade school and he said he was rowdy during that time. He dropped out of high school when he was sixteen but returned on his own initiative to complete the last two years because that was what he wanted to do. "I was wild and had a terrible temper, though I didn't do prison time." Once he set a house on fire for which he got a "bad woopin'" and add to that, he tried to drown a friend in a pool. His friend still remembers it but Franklin didn't until he was reminded. He completed a nine month security guard training program.

After three years in the swirl of his addictions, Franklin decided to get a grip on himself and confronted his dependence on cigarettes, alcohol and marijuana. He conquered his addiction to all three at one time. What a tremendous accomplishment and tribute to the power which is within him! He said his remaining addiction is to overeat. He admits he craves attention, approval and affection. There is a psychological theory that drug use is learned from interaction with others in the culture. His parents drank and sanctioned his behavior. He said his friends were abusers, too.

He became alienated from his mother because of her addictions. His "going clean" lost him that circle of friends and others in his family. The loss is still hard on him.

Franklin confided that he experienced physical and emotional abuse in his childhood and struggles daily against the tendency to revisit the same violence in his own adult relationships. Everyday interactions with the women in his life, his son and community were tinged with the rage that was still in him. This was not a unique tale that Franklin told. I heard it so many times over. Grown-ups, walking wounded.

He never married, but talked about a young woman he met who also was interested in jazz music. He said he gave her two pair of his favorite coveralls for which he paid $52.00 a piece at the Army Surplus store. When she was not highly thrilled at his gift, he said to her, "I gave you my most prized possessions!" Bewildered, he asked, "does a woman love more deeply than a man?" He candidly said he doesn't think he will ever get married because "I'm not good at promising. I can't please any woman."

Franklin's comfortable coping style was to fight or take flight. He was trying to reign-in his aggressive emotions. Currently, when he had a disagreement with his lady friend, he left her to keep from beating her instead of verbally trying to resolve the conflict. He grappled with his dominating, heavy-handed manner seeing that it got in his way at most every turn.

Franklin has one son five years old who is from a brief encounter. "I communicate with him occasionally but don't support him." He said he couldn't deny that the boy was his because "he has an exact resemblance to me. I would like to see the boy more often but it is too painful the way I get along with my son's mother's family. They have a lot to say when I show up." He wants to keep his son "in line" because he doesn't want the youngster to be a "cowboy" like he used to try to be. When asked if this meant beating him, he said, "if he needed it."

"He needs a strong hand" and explained he views fatherhood as being an enforcer and occasionally a playmate. "I didn't have a father when I was growing up so I can only imagine how I should be."

As hard as he tries, Franklin keeps running into barriers to regular employment due to a felony on his record. He has a police record dating back to his early twenties. Because of that, he cannot get a security guard job doing what he was trained to do. He may not own or carry a weapon. Also, that police record of a robbery, which he says he did not commit, keeps rearing its ugly head when potential employers announce that a police check is a part of the employment process. He lost a chance for a job at a local college just for that reason. When asked what the impact of his jail experience was, he said he was OK for jail but the robbery sentence changed him. He was more bitter. He fought more and his cell mate went to sleep on his bunk and never woke up. "That freaked me out!"

He was incarcerated at the Workhouse and Justice Center but never in prison. The longest time he was in jail was for three months. He said that proved to him they knew he really had not pulled the robbery. Shortly after he got released he saw the man who accused him of the crime and he told him, "Hey, mon (sic), you sent me in for something I didn't do." The man had him arrested for verbal abuse and he got ten more days. Franklin said one thing he learned in jail was that writing one's name on the wall means the prisoner will return. "I did and it got me ten more days." As a wild child, he said he has other arrests on his rap sheet, driving while intoxicated, driving without a license, drug abuse for marijuana, criminal damaging, and assault.

Franklin loves hard, physical work. He was connected with several temporary employment agencies which he called a couple of times every day. He had difficulty getting assignments where real construction was going on because he didn't have a car. He lost jobs in a couple of suburban communities for that reason. This is a recurring problem for inner city people who do not have independent transportation.

He worked for a non profit work-hardening company which did laborer jobs like tearing down old buildings. This particular boss goaded him, Franklin said, and constantly rode him on reducing his weight, on improving his work habits and focusing his attention span. He accepted correction and criticism and did not retaliate to his boss's remarks. Personally, though, he considered the prying questions and insults posed to him as racially discriminating. He revealed that the workers who belonged to the church that was running the project were paid two dollars more an hour than he was.

Franklin says he wants to be in more control of his life and to be able to support himself and have, as his mother often told him, "nice clothes, a car, a big apartment." He said he comes from a culture where the man's self respect, self-esteem and status is intimately bound with his ability to support his family. His role is financial and his status in the household depends strictly on his ability as a breadwinner. When a man is unable to carry out his role as a breadwinner, he falls a great distance in the estimation of himself, as well as his wife and children, the neighbors and community. I remembered a young woman who told me that she never let a man come to dinner at her place unless he brought a bag of groceries!

With his self esteem at rug level, he admitted that he was resigned to the misfortunes and lost opportunities which had befallen him over the years. Those human desires of wanting to have nice things got in the way of his work goals sometimes. He had a chance to interview for a job at one of the hospitals wouldn't go because he didn't have what he thought were the right kind of shoes.

I asked Franklin where he saw himself in five years. "I sure wouldn't be in Cincinnati! Wherever I am, I'll be doing painting, only I would be a supervisor and show my workers how to paint and work on ladders."

After a while, Franklin felt more comfortable with me and we were able to talk about racism and discrimination. One time he said he wished he had not been born black. I have let 'the man' take care of what needs to be done." I inquired what he meant by "the man". Did he mean his white bosses? He responded, "any boss!" He appears to be in awe of authority figures and craved authority and responsibility.

"I used to vote but don't anymore." He added, he feels disconnected, disenfranchised. "I stopped because I felt powerless. Look, I can hardly afford bus fare to go to work. Votes don't do me no good." When I asked if he was involved in civil rights has said, "No, I don't want to be intimidated." We talked about the gentrification of a street east of downtown which was threatening to take low income housing from "his people".

Then he asked, "Miss Joanne, (he wouldn't call me anything else) level with me. Would you change places and be a black woman? Though this was not the first time I was asked that question, it is always one that pulls me up short. Knowing what I know of the curve balls, unfairness and meanness that they have to confront every day, it is something I don't think I'd volunteer for. If I started out as an Afro American female, I probably would have thought everyone's life was like mine. For sure, I know I do not have the confidence or the strength of the beautiful African American women in my purview. I stand as a coward compared to the what I see our black women (and men) facing every day.

I asked Franklin what he is afraid of. He said, "Dying. Drugs. Cigarettes, Drinkin'. I fear I might lose somebody close to me." I pushed further, and asked what frustrates him the most and he shivered and answered, "My mother and family. Here I am in my thirties and she is still telling me what to do. And I know she is right. But I still lose my temper with her because I want to do things my own way." Musician Tom Wait has a song called "Keep the Devil Down in the Hole!" I could see Franklin stuffing those monsters back down in the hole!

Franklin appeared to be hyperactive and impulsive. He spoke loudly and put on a tough aire. Repeatedly he said "What's up, mon, (sic)? What be danglin'?" Over time, I could see he was trying to soften his manner, especially with the guests who frequented the soup kitchen.

Fast forward several years and Franklin had moved on. One Oktoberfest downtown, I was helping at a booth from which the kitchen was to receive the proceeds. He came up to me with his wife and little girl. In the sinking sun, I hardly recognized him. He looked calm, proud and wholesome.

"Fill me in, what has happened to you since you left us," I asked. I wasn't prepared for Franklin's late history. The story cascaded like watching an avalanche unfold from a distance. "You know I play the drums. I got on with a gospel band and we had a chance to go to Japan. We played over there, recorded our work, and man! I am a different guy! When we came back, I got a full time job with benefits at a laundry. Then, more good stuff happened to me. I met my wife here and she had a daughter." His pretty wife stood there quietly, shaking her head affirmatively. The little girl called him Daddy! "Finally, after we married, we bought a house up in College Hill. I am OK!"

"Franklin," I gushed, "You should be glowing with pride for yourself. It's your work! I am glad you found a way to meet your goals! It sounds like you hung in there to make your dreams become reality! You took control of your life! Listen to you! Getting to take your talent to Japan! I am SO proud of you!"

There were many questions I wished I could ask him. It was late afternoon and the russet sun seemed to cuddle around the downtown buildings. We were standing on Fountain Square shading our eyes. The crowd was becoming heavy. I was happy for any facts he wanted to share with me!
"Miss Joanne, you all helped me get there!" You treated me like I had possibilities!" I grinned and clapped, "You have to take the bow all by yourself!"

Pam Farrel said, "Perseverance makes impossible opportunities possible." Franklin said good-by and moved into the crowd with his arm around his wife and little girl in tow.

"ALMOST, MISS JOANNE, ALMOST!"

*Lannie wasn't clued
To the damage beer could take.
Too soon it took her.*

LANNIE MARSHALL

Lannie was a sweet little lady who seemed to live life in slow motion. She served coffee to the people when they first arrived in the morning. My guess was that Lannie, years back, was in the slow learner class. She had her own little place. Having a caring family wasn't enough to keep her from a dependency on alcohol. She wasn't confrontational but was street smart. She didn't hide her addiction and was very open about loving the taste and effect of her "40 ouncer". She must have had some on her Cheerios and washed down her lunch with it. We really never knew her any other way. Her slow manner of speaking was always polite, wrapped with a southern twist.

Since she was very small in stature it was easy to miss her in the crowd and she had a personality to go with her anonymity. She faded into the background, only emerging when she had good news. She was always tidy as was her work area.

Lannie loved bingo rub-offs. Each Wednesday after work she would purchase her two dollar card. She would get cards with a fist full of money from other workers, too, and when she returned from the deli, everybody scraped their cards together. Lannie seemed to know money. She would rest her arms on the kitchen's cool steel work table and carefully rub the ticket and declare her good fortune of a buck or two. I don't remember Lannie winning much, but that didn't stop her from trying again and again. She would always bring her losing card to me and happily declare, "Almost, Miss Joanne! Almost!" And I would compliment her on her persistence and good faith. She would have fifteen rows that were missing one number and never once did she get irritated or discouraged. Evidently she could read numbers and letters well, but words not so much.

Everyone liked her easy, pleasant temperament. She was genuinely grieved for when, one afternoon, her friends came rushing in to say Lannie, who was a frequent flier (one who was on a first name basis with the Fire Department ambulance squad) wouldn't be back. She dropped mid street with a heart attack and couldn't be revived. She died shortly after.

Death seemed to hover over the kitchen. Nonetheless, most of us were surprised when we would lose one of our people. Even though it occurred often, the surprise element could have been the youth of the deceased. So often the men would grieve the loss of their male friends who many times were shot and killed.

In spite of the frequency of death among our customers, it may cause doubt in some, but there was a spirit of hope. Hope that someone would be able to break from the spiral of violence, of unemployment and of discouragement. The harsh lifestyle, the clutch of addictions and the rude way people had to live snagged people far too early. I remember someone saying, "There are no old drunks."

It took us a while to get over losing Lannie as we had become fond of her. Her family gave her a wonderful funeral at the church where she had had the proud honor of being a "nurse," one who wore a special white outfit to assist others with needs during a service. A bus took mourners to the cemetery and returned them for a jolly celebration at the funeral home. Her sisters and brothers, who lived away from the neighborhood and who led successful lives, came in soon after and brought a memorial donation in her honor.

A sweet memory I have of her is of one late summer afternoon when the sun sliced between the huddled buildings. The kitchen was locked for the day. We said our good-byes and I watched Lannie who was totally comfortable with herself, ambling down the lane wearing a wicker flower basket upside down on her head. The handle was under her chin. "God love it!" my Grandma used to say!

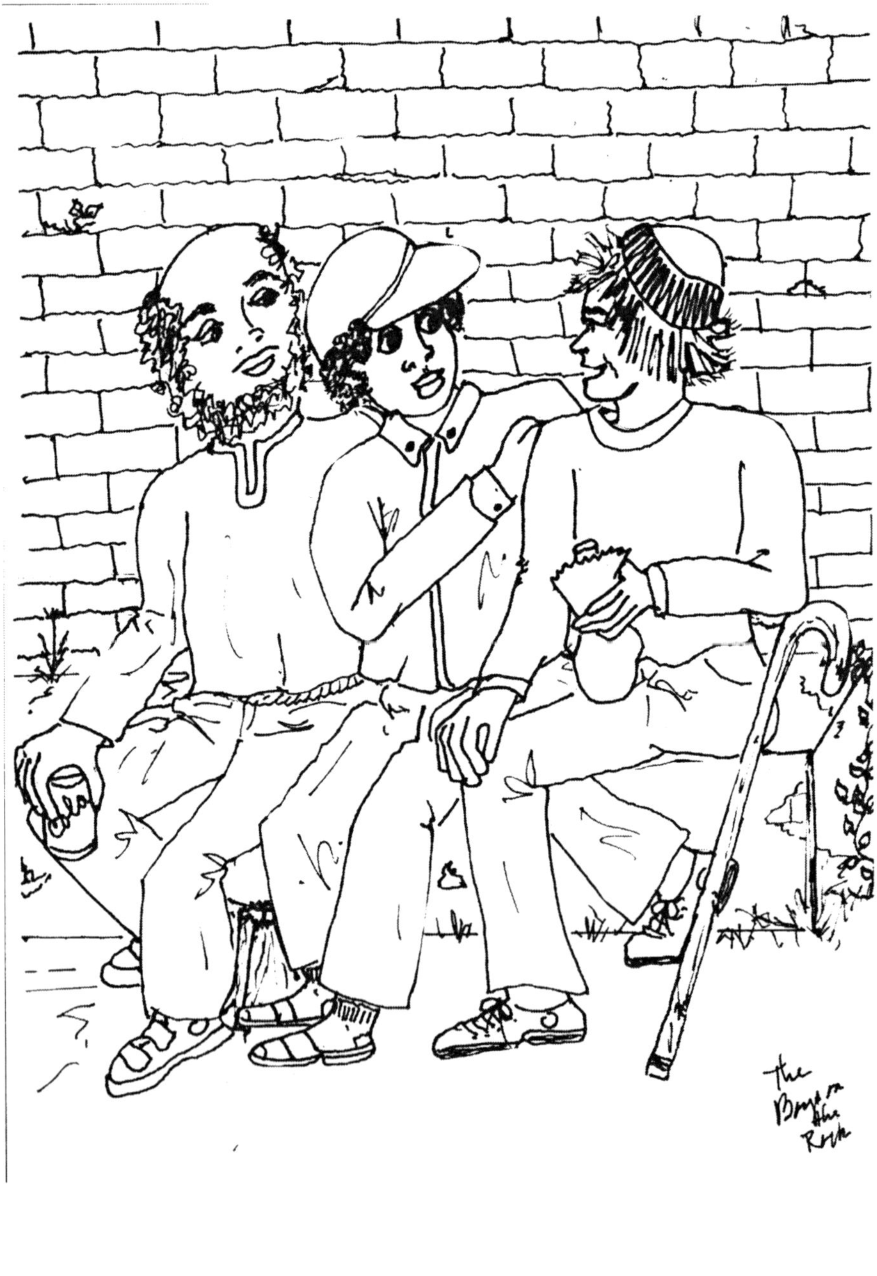

"THE BOYS ON THE ROCK"

His russet skin is leathery.
The plastic orange day glow hat is soiled and cracked.
At 78, he shuffles into the kitchen, smiling.
He tries to keep his poverty a secret
As well as his hard life behind him.
He never begs or acts pathetic.
But you should see him grin
When he gets a private little treat!
Just a bit of something for his overactive sweet tooth.

CORY FREEMAN

One of our favorite customers was Cory Freeman, a 77 year old African American man. Affable, cooperative, and quiet. Who wouldn't choose to engage this smiling, gentle old man? He lived a block away in a dark, bug infested rent subsidized senior building. We thought the building should be condemned because the halls were very narrow and dim. The elevator jolted to the second floor. "Don't take your purse or lean against anything or sit down," I was warned on my first visit. The drywall was pulling away from the joists and ceiling beams. Roaches and vermin owned the place. It looked like it had never been painted. I wandered how it ever passed inspections because it looked the same to me every time I'd visit.

Many of the elderly residents were disabled, but it certainly was not accessible. We worried for them, should there ever be a fire in that tinderbox. Narrow halls made it difficult moving in or out. Many seniors were smokers. Cory knew he could have had his lunch brought to him with the home delivery program where volunteers walked their lunches to the aged residents (instead of driving them!) several times a week. But Cory chose to join the kitchen crowd and experience the hub bub and maybe go home with a few treats. He wore the same cracked plastic day glow orange baseball cap and unmatched clothes every day. He said he liked to watch the workers serving the meal and grinned brightly when one would hand him a brown bag with bakery goods, candy or personal items. He would never ask for anything himself.

Cory was born to married parents in Providence, Kentucky. He was raised by his working mother. She would take housekeeping jobs as far away as St. Louis during which time his father's grandparents often cared for him on their farm. He said he didn't mind being in their care because he always had enough to eat. What he DID mind was having to "slop" the pigs and getting his clothes soiled. His little town was segregated as was the high school in Princeton, Kentucky where he left at age 16 to help his mother. Nearly seven decades later he still regretted leaving without a diploma. He believed that it was his not completing his education that held him back far more than racism or discrimination. He said he had never heard about such things until he moved to the big city. "It wasn't a problem when it was just us blacks!"

Cory went into the Air Force when he was 18 and spent three years as a waiter-cook at the Louisville Officers Club. He wished he had stayed in but left because they offered him money to leave. "That was dumb," he added. Throughout his life he held a variety of construction, laundry, meat packing and railroad jobs. "How I wish I had stayed with the railroad. I'd have a pretty good pension now!" He said he had a good disposition and got along with bosses and workers just fine. His dream was to open his own business *selling stuff* but never had enough money to get started.

In 1940 he married his only wife. They separated three years later. He supported his son and daughter by sending money every week. They live in Cleveland now with a half dozen grandchildren whom he never sees, consequently, he never thinks about them much. He grinned and added that he never remarried but "always kept a woman."

With Cory such an easy going guy, it was surprising to hear him say the recurring themes in his life were "drinkin' and jail." His great regret was that and smoking. He started those habits in high school when he'd get with the *boys*. He didn't even like the taste of the booze but said the buzz felt good. Then, without any help, he stopped drinking four years ago. "But I wish I had stopped 20 years ago. I'd get so sick I'd wish I could die. I'd go to Alcoholics Anonymous meetings by myself but never stopped. Now I just drink pop or water even when I'm with *the boys*. It don't bother me none that they are drinkin' and I'm not."

He said he always had a lot of white friends who actually treated him better than some blacks. But when they'd drink together, their tongues would loosen and there would always be someone who would call him *nigger*. "I wouldn't get mad and fight. I always treated people right. I tried to forget the bad times," he whispered. "I kept a smile on my face. It was the only way to survive." It didn't take much to understand he had experienced far more negative experiences than he chose to talk about. He declared quite firmly, "I know discrimination when I sees it. *Black* is just a name."

I asked him what he and his friends said about discrimination and racial prejudice and he said they talked about it a little, then every day, they'd say less and less. Cory confided that he found the civil rights movement frightening and didn't know which side to be on. "Martin Luther King was wrong to do it all by hisself. He shoulda let the courts settle it. It's a miracle that more blacks didn't get killed. I didn't go for marchin; cause it didn't seem like the way to do it. Killin' Kennedy was the worstest thing!" He became emotional when he added, "I was outraged and hurt."

In retrospect, Cory mused that he didn't guess he had any successes except stopping drinking. "I just do the best I can one day at a time because that is all that's promised. You don't know if you'll get more or not. I don't have any unfinished business." He accepted nearly eight decades of life with a certain contentment and no regrets. "I just moved along. I wish I could have lived with a woman but it was hard to find one to trust!"

Without a wimper, the losses piled on Cory, suffering from lack of a father, from an unstable family situation, entrapping addictions, disengaging from his marital relationship and parenthood and lack of an education. One wonders how stuffing and silencing any reaction to slings and arrows diminished him. He viewed his paternal responsibilities as being fulfilled by sending money to his ex wife. He proved he could conquer the "monkey on his back" alcoholism on his own. But sixty years smoking had done awful physical damage to him. He had to get up every seven to eight minutes and light a cigarette, inhale and stub it out. He'd start coughing and spitting. "I wish I had never started. I can't seem to stop like I did the drinkin'."

As a distraction to his discomfort, Cory said he "used to play the piano by ear real good. I don't have no cravin' for it now but I'd still mess with it if I could. I'd try."

When asked how he spends his evenings, he said he listens to the Reds' game, takes naps and likes "bein' with the boys on the rock." That is one of two cement planters fronting what was once a near-by furniture store near the city's street market area. It was there that Cory sat with the old men of the neighborhood as they hugged their bagged bottles talking their talk "til the shade moves." Each was a superman when it was his turn to taut the highlights of his life.

Cory was sent to a nursing home not long after we had our chat. His only visitor was the kitchen's director who would bring him flowers and candy. He died of lung cancer.

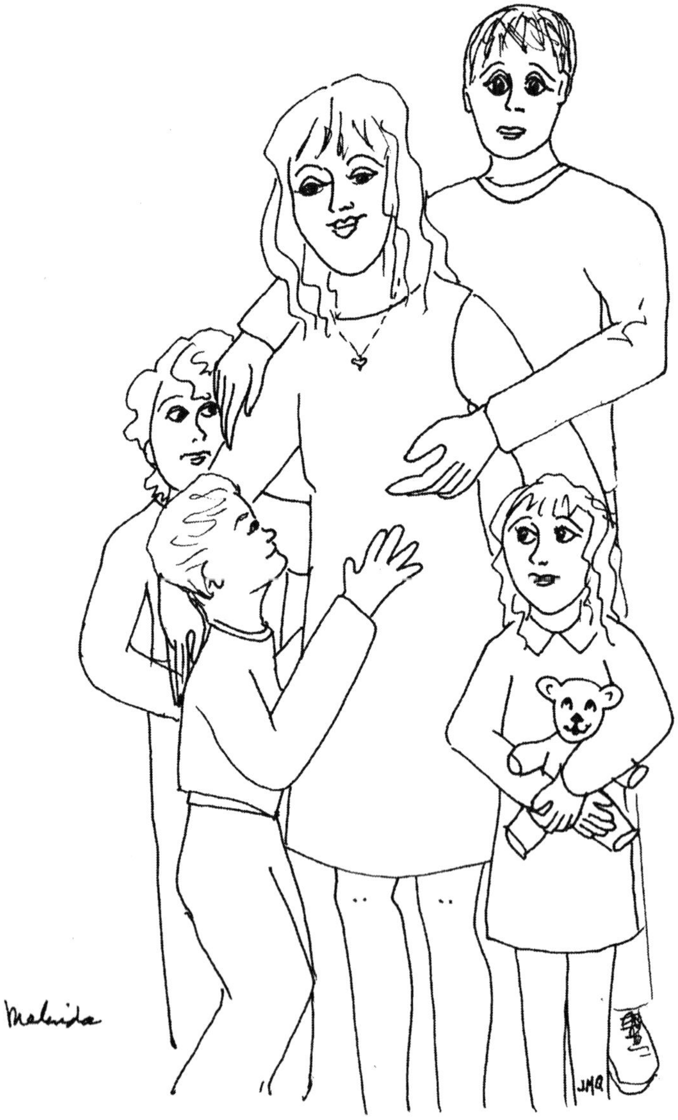

"When everything is coming your way, you are in the wrong lane."

There was no clue life could turn inside out. A mom faced the crisis of her life!

MELINDA DONAHUE

Homelessness can happen to anyone. Melinda worked for a major manufacturing company in middle management. The company was cutting back and giving long term employees buy outs. She had several grade school aged children, and was happy that it brought an opportunity to home school them and be a full time Mom. Both she and her husband were college graduates. He, too had a professional job for a construction firm. She thought she was fortunate to have the health care benefit follow her into retirement. It even covered her husband and children. Life had been good to them up to that point. They were making extra payments on their home and were able to provide enrichments to the family.

Lightning struck with her getting a cancer diagnosis. The health insurance was not as comprehensive as it needed to be. She had stage four breast cancer. Her husband Paul, in a shocking, unforewarned moment, lost his job. The company was going out of business. At first, though crushed by the side tracking of their goals, the couple thought they would weather the problem and see their way through it like they always did.

The financial cushion they were so pleased with began to deplete. There was no stop to the drain. Their savings disappeared. Co pays and non covered services and hospital bills accrued. Soon their assets dwindled and the liabilities mushroomed. A job that met Paul's previous salary was not forthcoming.

Trying to get Melinda's disease into remission took a long time. At one point she was so thin and ill she weighed as much as her young son. This was not in their life plan. As the family's financial resources dissipated, they began to tap other aspects like insurance loans and using their credit cards. It was not their habit to spend money like that. It took years to get over having to have their house foreclosed.

That little family became homeless. Where does one suburban family go without an income with three kids? Our families love us, but most do not have space or income to take us in. They found a place to rent. But the house was later sold and they were again reminded of their status.

They moved to a second house in an area unknown to them. In a year, the same thing happened. A friend offered to have the family stay with them. Once more, that did not last long term. A second friend invited the parents but not the kids. That friend became disenchanted with their house guests and asked them to move again. Finding homes was miserable for everybody.

Then came crushing news: there was a recurrence of Melinda's illness. Paul's continuing, discouraging job options offered little to them except low paying labor assignments. They tried to be positive and hopeful but their experience was bleak and depressing. They finally were able to get an apartment through the housing authority and become reunited. Word got out and help from friends, family, foundations and organizations helped with some of the debts. But none of the help provided ongoing income that was so needed.

Recently, after ten years of treatment, surgeries, drugs and therapies, Melinda succumbed to her illness. Will the family ever recover any stability? Who would have predicted such a string of family tragedies, especially catastrophic illness, homelessness and indebtedness for that family? It was no soap opera. It had nothing to do with inadequacies or mismanagement. Fate had its way with a good, hard working and very ordinary family.

Paul recently got a full time job working for a non profit. He probably will never recover his lost income, but he does not complain, thankful he has a job with some benefits. The children, now motherless, and Paul now a widower, are working hard to reconnect and re-shape their lives.

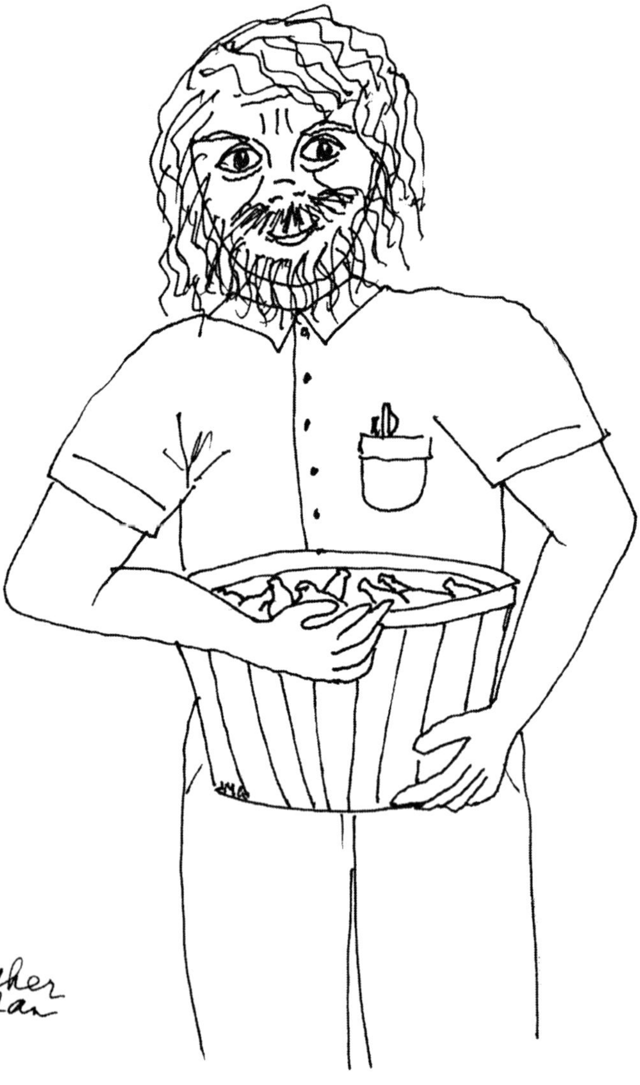

Preacher Man

THE PREACHER MAN

**His chickens weren't
exactly rubber but still
were inedible.**

JOSIAH PETERS

There was a deference given to the elderly Reverend whenever he came to lunch. With both in poor health, he always brought his frail, sweet wife Rose with him wherever he went. He didn't want to leave her alone. She was older than he and they talked about how they were still very much in love with each other. My guess is he was at least 80 having been married to Rose almost 60 years.

The Reverend would easily bring out his fire and brimstone sermon, triggered by any topic. Knowing his old fashioned values, the fellows behaved around him. He drove a dilapidated rusty van which, how should we say it, was highly disorganized. It was crammed with unrelated items from who knows where, like torn tennis sneakers and shabby books, soiled clothing, potatoes with eyes staring back at us and toys. Crates had nondescript contents draping through the slats.

About once a week he would pull up to the door, so proud he had something to give the kitchen. The van door would slide open with a screech and he would motion, as if to say "TA DA! Presenting . . . **some pale, withering chickens!** The odor warned us before our eyes fell on his wilted, unrefrigerated poultry which were drooping inside a dirty five gallon bucket. We would gulp and rave about our good fortune, accepting the gift as graciously as we could. We never did know who was the donor of this pathetic stuff. Maybe he rescued it from the butcher shop trash can, I don't know.

After the Reverend drove down the lane, the chickens were laid to rest in our dumpster.

Rachelle

"NOT ONLY IS LIFE A BITCH BUT IT IS ALWAYS HAVING PUPPIES."

Adrienne Gustoff

This lady guest had a secret life we didn't realize. Much lost!

RACHELLE WINSTON

There was a gentility about Rachelle. She was about seven years younger than I but looked beyond my years. It didn't used to be that way! There was a softness and gracefulness to her, along with what we always thought was common sense. When I met her she was living in a tiny third story walk-up apartment and was stretching her small income by walking to the soup kitchen each day. Though her finances were limited, she had shelter and the basics of life.

Rachelle injured herself lifting a patient and could no longer work in the direct care units of a health care facility. She felt overwhelmed by new testing requirements for aides that were imposed with State certification and that added to her problems. The Facility transferred her to working in the dietary department but that also carried with it physical demands and her strength was no longer there. She also had low reading ability.

She told us, she always felt good when she was at the Kitchen. We were always glad to see her. Rachelle would participate in the activities and play cards daily in the back room with her friends. The staff gave her and the other guests affirmation. Her cheery round Granny face balanced her full figure. Like so many of the guests, she always wore a hat. Things could be hidden under the *chapeau du jour.*

People often doubt that those who are poor are really in need if they are overweight. Their meager budgets only allow them to purchase foods that are starchy and filling, like pasta, cheap bread, French fries, and peanut butter. The healthier foods, like lean meats, vegetables, grains and fruits come with a higher price. Lack of resources, physical exercise, appropriate shoes and transportation keep them from getting healthy activity. When I was at the kitchen only 1% of the 350 people a day had cars.

Rachelle stopped coming to the kitchen for awhile and we thought she either moved or worse, had died. Her friends were reluctant to give any reason why she didn't show. Finally, one day she came in and immediately I said to her, "We have missed you. Are you all right? You are wasting away. Have you been sick?" She confided that she was homeless. I couldn't hide my shock on that response! How did that happen to one of our star customers? Usually, I tried to leave the door open should they wish to tell me more.

She had appeared to be one of the stable guests who came nearly every day. At least, we thought, she had a consistent income. She was spare in discussing how her homelessness came to be, but finally confided that she got into crack cocaine and it made her "lose everything!" I wouldn't have guessed Rachelle would fall for it, but I didn't press her for details. Alcohol, maybe, but not the wicked hard stuff! It was generous of her to let me know what was really happening to her. All I could say was, "Oh, Rachelle!"

One thing I noticed while working in the inner city was that there is so much peer pressure. Rachelle's situation indicated that it was not just youth who fell prey to taking awful risks with their wellbeing. What was the desperation that drove her to risk herself with deadly chemicals? Seniors were equally as vulnerable and dependent. Their options were even more narrow than younger people. In a small community people need friends and crave a social life. Their problems are extreme, and erasing them even for a little while may seem like a pretty good idea.

It was hard to see Rachelle as a recovering addict. She didn't fit any of the stereotypes of inner city druggies. We had no idea what demons drove her to partake. We didn't know how physically miserable she was or if alcoholism reduced her impulse control. She was old enough to know crack cocaine was a dead end street. Rachelle's heart was affected by her drug use and with her budget depleted, she lost the only comfort and safety she had. She never was able to recover her old stability. She finally found a couple of rooms she could afford but they were four or five miles away in a strange neighborhood. She kept coming to the kitchen even though she had to lay out money for car fare. As a welcome back present I gave her my last four precious bus tokens that would save her a few cents.

Bus tokens were like gold coins and were given when we had them available and then only for a good and specific reason such as getting up to the hospital. But we knew for some, they were worth trading for whatever change was needed that day. I questioned myself whether I should give them to her for she might just sell them on the way to the bus stop. I decided Rachelle needed some trust and a break.

"LIFE IS WHAT HAPPENS WHEN YOU ARE MAKING PLANS"

John Lennon

In the dark, she's down for the count, but will bounce back with some outside help.

MAUREEN FIELDING

One morning my first client was Maureen Fielding, who didn't fit the stereotype of our guests. She looked stressed like many did, but her demeanor was more sophisticated. She wore tidy and well tailored clothes and had lovely, comfortable shoes. Her carrot colored hair was cut well. Nonetheless, Maureen was homeless.

She was married to a judge and had lived in an outer county. Her husband found a younger woman with whom to share his up-scale life. He had a network of attorney friends who declined to take her case. Her husband had found a way to take every resource she had, including a car, house keys, and bank funds. Fortunately a friend rescued her and gave her shelter and safety for a few days.

"How did you get here?" I asked. She had taken the bus to us when someone suggested she talk to me. "Where do I go from here?" she cried. "I don't have a job. I have nowhere to live. I have no money. I don't have transportation. I don't know how this all happened."

We made an inventory of things Maureen did have, among those, a teaching degree and a determination to pull herself out of this miserable trough. Because she was a spunky sort, I knew she would be one of the few who would be able to sprout wings and become independent. I gave her some bus tokens, a bag of personal items, and a handful of possible resources to jump start her life.

At this moment in her life, she was deeply vulnerable, but still, Maureen bore a dignity not often seen in those who are being oppressed. She stood in the lunch line and did not look frightened by the throng of men who were crowded in the hall. I saw that she struck conversations with different people. Her strength would carry her, I believed.

This happened in the days before we all carried cell phones. I wondered how Maureen was fairing. I had invited her back to work with her some more, but had to wait 'til she returned to the kitchen. A few weeks later she called me to say she had a job as a grade school teacher in a suburban private school. She found a divorce attorney in Cincinnati who was willing to go up against her husband, and soon she would move to a small apartment. Maureen embodied documentation that anyone can become homeless. This story is a reminder that homelessness is not isolated to a specific category of people. Unlike most others, it also has a quick and happy ending.

I remember when we did a survey once, only one of 75 of the respondents had a college degree. That educational underpinning can be the bedrock of future success but it isn't a given. Not everybody can finish college. Some are limited cognitively, some have physical or mental conditions that make it more challenging to bring about. Some have not yet identified or tapped their gifts. Some have one or more impediments to being qualified for a job or housing. Most of the time, ending homelessness had no simple answers.

Bringing an end to the hopelessness of homelessness requires sweat and equity. Finally, obtaining a roof over one's head entails a detailed plan and the means to maintain it. It is more than a bus stop shelter. Most of our people who finally did work their way into their own place had some awesome barriers to overcome, but they kept chugging to climb over them and with determination, discipline and with a lot of help from their friends they were able to end a most painful stage in their lives.

Sometimes things work out differently than planned. A young single woman with a pre-school-aged-son was taking college classes, working part time and trying to pay for child care and shelter. It was hard going for her. Her nerves were frayed and resources were thin. Her goal was to get a degree and improve their lives. Each time I saw her, I encouraged her to keep visualizing her graduation. I would give her school supplies, boy clothes, food, personal items to help keep her afloat. She found an opportunity for a much better job and made the decision to quit school. She said when the dust settled she would return to school, but found it necessary to grab at the chance when it presented itself. She met her goal in another way.

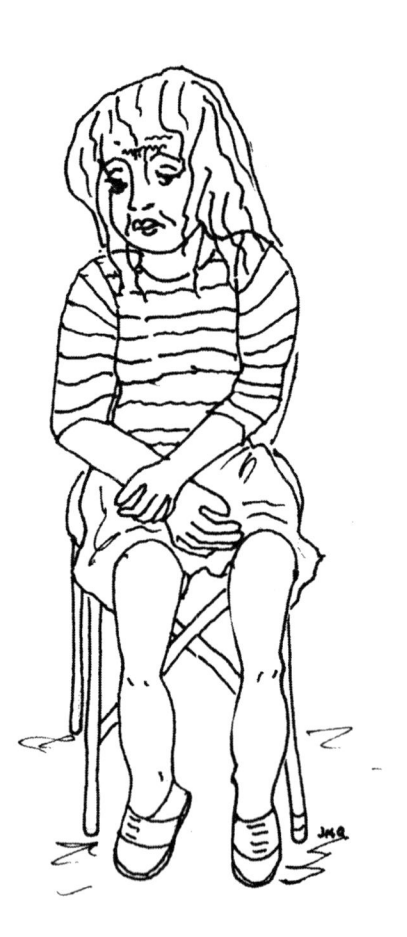

Lilly

ONE MORE NIGHTMARE ON ELM STREET

**It isn't supposed
to be this way. A girl's life
de-railed and ruined.**

LILLY STONER

With apologies to Freddy Krueger, all three of his movies, 12 novels and every comic book and spin off. This is a story of a needy child who happened to live on the real Elm Street near by and who had real night terrors that disturbed what little peace she had in her life. My hope was that she never saw or heard anything to do with Freddie. Lilly Stoner was ten years old and participated in different programs offered by the kitchen.

Over the years I heard brutal stories from different clients that to this minute are crystal clear in my memory. Some of the grown people we were working with and serving in the kitchen received violent abuse in their youth. In whispering voices they would tell me about their cigarette burns, being beaten with belts, switches, ropes and boards while tethered to a bedstead or post, being taught to drink when they were four years old, being locked in cellars or closets, and oh, so many, with sexual abuse all by people they knew and trusted. Not all of the violence toward them was from guardians, but happened in school. And this is an incomplete list of violations to innocents. Many in that group suffered under parents or elders who were alcoholics or were drug addicted. Cross that with poverty and difficulty in school and you have a lethal potion.

There were also wonderful people whom we served who were survivors of tragic assaults to their souls and bodies from when they were children. But they chose to not revisit them on their progeny. But too real in that group of adults are people who were broken in critical ways and who self medicate or try to salve their everlasting pain in self destructive ways. Some don't know there are other ways to raise children save the one they experienced.

Most of the kids in our programs were cooperative and fun to work with. But one in particular was a thorn called Lilly. I looked at this pretty ten year old girl with a great deal of concern. She would look everyone in the eye with simmering resentment and anger as if to say "Try me!" She kept her eye lids squeezed together with only a slit between her curly black lashes. Her lips would be pursed tightly together. There was a sad and sullen look glazing her face. She was physically maturing ahead of her peers. I looked at her thinking she must have feelings of rug level self value stewing in a cauldron of rage. She had the vocabulary of a longshoreman. How did she learn these behaviors with only a decade on the planet? After a few run-ins with her I learned bits of her history. This young person had more awful things happen to her in her first years of life, than most people have in a lifetime.

When Lilly was a preschooler, her birth father was murdered in this very neighborhood. Secret things must have happened to this child to stir up such meanness and distrust. Several times, she was suspended from our children's after school group and sent to me. Now I was not the disciplinarian and dealing with naughty children is not my strong suit. I knew her from the summer program where she caused so much chaos that even the top administrator would brush her hands together and say the child was hopeless. "The girl must be possessed." I wonder if Lilly heard the woman say that because when the instructor got close to our girl to talk to her, the girl deliberately threw up on the teacher's shoes. The instructor was a religious teacher with many years experience with all sorts of children. No one could handle Lilly.

While Lilly was showing us how miserable she was, the other children were seeing cows for the first time. They were afraid to walk in the grass and wouldn't sit on a blanket because a fierce daddy long legs would get them.

Such an unhappy girl. She must have felt miserable. Severe behavior problems were isolating her and skewing her childhood experience in negative directions in warp speed. Her teachers in school said they resented having to have Lilly in their classes as it took all their attention from the other students. Consult with the mother was difficult because she, too was an angry woman who would or could not hear what the teachers were saying about her daughter. She would not answer the phone or the door when the teacher would call or social worker would visit. Amazingly, one time, when Lilly was sitting in my office on *time out,* she told me about her nightmares. "Scary" ones that caused her to waken and try to run crying from her room. One summer night, she wakened from a terrifying dream and ran to the window trying to jump from the third floor apartment to the cement courtyard below. A cousin happened to be staying there that night and prevented the tragedy. Once Lilly disclosed this terrifying tale to me it was as if she sneezed and went back to being herself. She hummed to herself. I tried to use empathy with her, but she put herself out of reach. I tried to draw her out but couldn't recapture that intimate moment.

Disruptive behaviors like classroom disturbances, throwing objects, disobedience, talking back, making noises and running in the halls, cursing, messing up the blackboards, kicking the trash can, stirring conflict with the children and vandalism emerged, getting more serious with each birthday. She would lie, but stealing hadn't been yet been reported.

Lilly's mother had male friends stay overnight when the child was home. She sometimes left Lilly in their care. Lilly said she did not like these men but would never go into detail why she felt that way. Once she was incarcerated at juvenile hall and her mother went to see her. The mom demanded her man friend remove his belt and she said she beat Lilly unmercifully, right in front of the (stoic) guard while screaming she didn't like being embarrassed by her daughter!

Parts of Lilly were excellent. She could sing. She loved to sing. She was good at painting and drawing. Why didn't someone take a hold of those gifts and use them therapeutically to pull her out of the whirlpool she was in? I decided the next time Lilly was sent to me, using art would be where we would start. Lilly came into my life so seldom that I didn't get a chance to tap the positive side of her. I did share this new knowledge about her to anyone whom I knew was working with her.

Lilly had learning deficits. She couldn't read well and math was a disaster. It was unclear if she had ever been assessed for her learning and behavioral handicaps.

The neighborhood where she lived was dense in subsidized housing complexes, treeless and overpopulated. Did she ever have a chance? Even with only occasional interactions with this child, anyone of us knew she was on a one way trip to disaster and needed strong intervention immediately.

Was Lilly safe in her home and neighborhood? Was she being abused? I needed something tangible to get her protective help. What were the seeds of her anger? Who could get through to the mother? Would a placement in a behavioral class be appropriate? In addition to therapy and a structured program, perhaps giving her a mentor, someone whom she couldn't intimidate, someone who was steady and could be affirming might be valuable to her. Lilly kept a lot of us up at night even when she wasn't there. She needed someone who would unlock her secrets and save her.

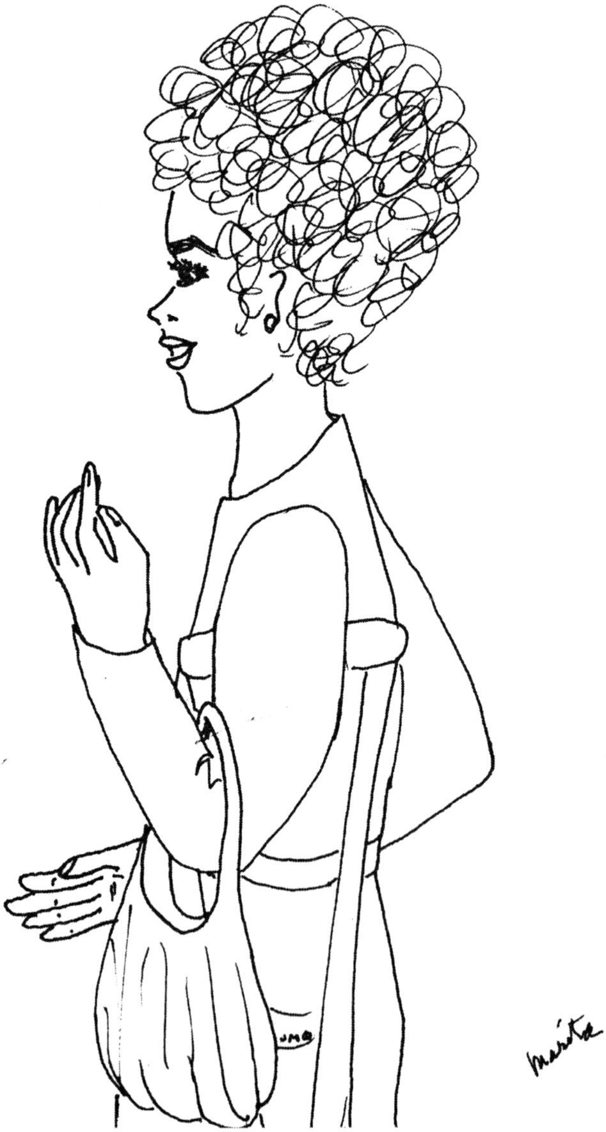

WITH EYES THAT SEE AROUND CORNERS

*Her career stunted,
an accident changed her course.
She asked us for help.*

MARITA HELLMAN

Marita was a large woman who carried herself with dignity. It wasn't hard to imagine her in a business suit. She was very comfortable with herself and knew her needs. Injured on the job, she was waiting the decision on her Supplemental Security Disability Income (SSDI) application.

It just killed her to have to use a cane. She was living without any income which was especially painful for this woman who had been self-sufficient and who loved new things. She hadn't been making mega bucks, but she was able to take care of her expenses and a bit more. Coming to a soup kitchen must have been really a trial for her. Her knee, elbow and back were injured badly in an industrial accident.

In addition to adjusting to chronic pain and the knowledge that she had a permanent injury, she had to get an attorney. Then she had to go through the business of getting the company to acknowledge the accident. Meeting her everyday needs was the common thread through her ordeal.

Fortunately, she was living in a new subsidized apartment and she had no rent once the manager recertified her in the zero rent category. But the need for food and other necessities created stress for which she would seek relief at the soup kitchen. Beyond the daily meal, sometimes I could help her, sometimes, not. I encouraged her to seek temporary help from her relatives which, I knew, was hard for her to do.

Like some other needy clients, she tried to meet as many of her needs at the kitchen as she could with one-stop shopping. She asked me for personal items and as I opened the drawer, she saw other things she wanted and said she needed. Usually, I would have little packages prepared ahead of time with whatever personal items we had on hand. I would keep a cover over the things in the drawer and a bag over the items on the open shelf, but that morning, I had an early appointment and didn't finish preparing for my morning clients.

"Oh, give me that belt, and the laundry soap and the deodorant and socks and the comb and the . . . mmmmm, is that shampoo? Give me some of that. Oh, and I need a toothbrush and lots of toothpaste. You've gained some weight haven't you? And I'd like to have some candy."

"I can appreciate that you have run short on a lot of things but I have to share what we have with a lot of people who are in a similar situation as you," I told her and pared her list to several of the things she requested. I knew she would be back soon and I needed to stretch the kitchen's resources.

Marita would never think of stealing. Think of the desperation that can lead to it. It was amazing how quickly clients could assess what was available. And take advantage of a possibility. People seemed to have the ability to see around corners and in cracks of the door. Acting quickly was the way to get what was needed. On the very few times I actually saw something being stolen, it was in a flicker of a second and the reaction to the availability was instantaneous. Of course that situation had to be confronted right away, and I'd say, "I saw you take the . . . . I'd like it back." Most of the time, people were embarrassed and apologetic. But I do remember how one woman acted like I was interrupting her adventure. I learned that sometimes people worked together, one as a diversion the other as the thief. Was this born of need or want? The things stolen were rarely expensive things, but were meant for the group or for an appropriate person.

Knives couldn't be left out for a second. If we ever had a metal detector at the door it would have been squawking all the time. One day, a clerk at the local supermarket called me and asked for a food gift certificate like the one she had cashed for a customer. That is one of the times I said I was out of them when I wasn't. It was only occasionally that I was given food gift certificates, and there had to be a heck of a need before they were given out. It might have been nice, certainly easier, to not have to be so stringent with the resources.

Endless lines of clients would stand outside the office door even though there were no appointments open and there was a sign saying we were out of resources. That meant no groceries, tokens, rent assistance, vouchers for birth certificates and/or id cards. They must have believed that I was saving something for them in spite of the notice. I hated when I was out of everything. Stretching the finite resources through the month was tough. It was stressful when people with true needs sat before me and there was no way to help. I'd offer to give them a referral to whatever organization was doing business in their category.

When I said I was out of tokens, they would say, "But what will I do?" We made no commitment or advertised the kitchen would meet everybody's needs. The clients assumed our help and that was a lot of pressure. "I have go to the doctor or hospital, or have a job interview. I only need two, just two!" It seemed similar to a game kids play, "but plu-eeze, Mom, can't I have . . . ?" I said *no* more often than *yes*. I would say no if I had helped the person recently. I said no if I knew the client had a regular income.

There was one day that stands out in memory. It was a couple days before Christmas. From nowhere, schools and organizations began dropping off toys for our parents to give to their kids. There was a parade of autos with open trunks lined up outside. I had never requested any organization to donate to us but the cars kept coming. Several parents had asked me previously for help. They were taken care of by volunteers. But we were not prepared for the bounty that about to befall us. It was like the loaves and fishes. Word obviously went around the neighborhood. Moms begged for "just one toy, please, just one!" When the last mother left, the toys stopped coming. The next year, any toys that were donated went to special programs and we referred parents on to them. Usually parents needed to register ahead of time and document need. Some charged a minimal amount, some had other requirements.

It was rare that we could help with an entire need. The monthly budget for helping with rent and utilities would barely cover one person's amount. But I would break it down to smaller amounts so we could help maybe eight to ten people. With the clothing budget, I could get one pair of work shoes a month. Any time there was a connection I referred the client on to them. Like a child's coat could be found at the Neediest Kids of All.

But back to Marita. It takes a long time until social security delivers its decision. For months she and I would spar over things that she wanted. Finally, she stopped coming and I learned only by accident that she had been approved for SSDI. She later said she forgot to let me know.

Part Four

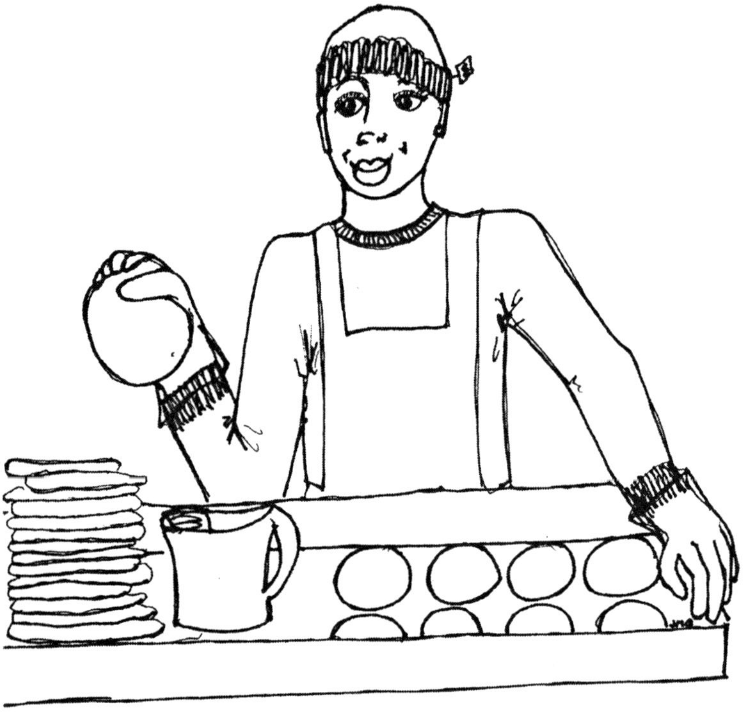

STATUS SYMBOLS

In the soup kitchen,
small phenomenas showed themselves.
The style of the day changed daily.
One morning I looked over the steam table to see
31 hungry men each wearing baseball caps with price tags.
Like Minnie Pearl, I thought,
but she was before their time.
Every hat was adjusted and worn with a slight but individual style.
Another day, navy and black woolen longshoreman type hats
kept them warm.
Again, each was fixed a tad differently from the others.
On a warm day, it was interesting to see how many unique ways a large handkerchief could be folded and knotted on our diner's heads.
Silent solidarity.
Yes, our men wore their hats in the house.
It kept them from being lost or stolen.
But the most respected fellow
was the one who didn't follow his peers.
He was the most envied.
He wore a worn leather tool belt burdened with heavy metal tools.
He had a job!

Today

TODAY

It's a puzzlement.
A juggling act.
Balancing the work of the day
with meeting human needs.
Soap. Gloves. Hats. Pencils. Socks.
Coats. Rent. Teeth. Teeth? Band Aids.
Bags. Postage stamps. A blanket. Aspirins. Cooking oil.
Condoms. (Whoops! Try the clinic!)
Bus fare. Light bulbs. Work Shoes. Underpants.
Sometimes I feel like I am being stoned to death with popcorn.
And other times I feet like I just nipped at therir issues.
"I want your earrings!:
"My husband is beating me again!"
"My son still can't read."
"I need a little sugar!" Hmmm!
"I am out of meat!"
"I got turned down by SSI."
"He cut in line."
Stir the pot.

Is there enough for a second helping?
It's all in a day's work.
"I'm pregnant."
"I have to buy tools for this job and I don't have any money."
"I got a job but I don't have a way to get there."
Trying to hold on to who I am.
Being REAL. Being PRESENT.
Trying to make a difference.
A delicate balance.
A test of mettle.
I just respond as best I can.

Gorilla warfare

GORILLA WARFARE

The police found him wrestling with a rather pickled young man
one dusty evening in Over The Rhine.
Right in the middle of the street.
The report said, "Check on a gorilla overcoming a man."
"Yeah, sure!"
But there he was!
Gorilla 3; Man 0!
"Thank goodness, you got here in time!" the man slurred.
"He just about got the best of me!"
They both got arrested.
The man-sized stuffed animal primate is doing his time hanging around
as the mascot of the local soup kitchen.

Body Count

BODY COUNT

I took my own survey, several times that month.
The measure of Black to White
of who came to dinner.
Fifteen percent of our guests at the soup kitchen
were Caucasian.
The rest were of other American origins.
Afro, over represented in the homeless population,
Indians and Mexicans.
Who says there is no racism in our city?
To keep people in poverty.
In ignorance.
In soup kitchens.
That's too easy.
Too bad.
All it seems
that the men talk about
over their bread and butter is
work.
They want it.
They need it.
Nobody hears that.
It's easier to be a social Darwin and blame the messenger.
Poverty sucks
the lifeblood from these people.

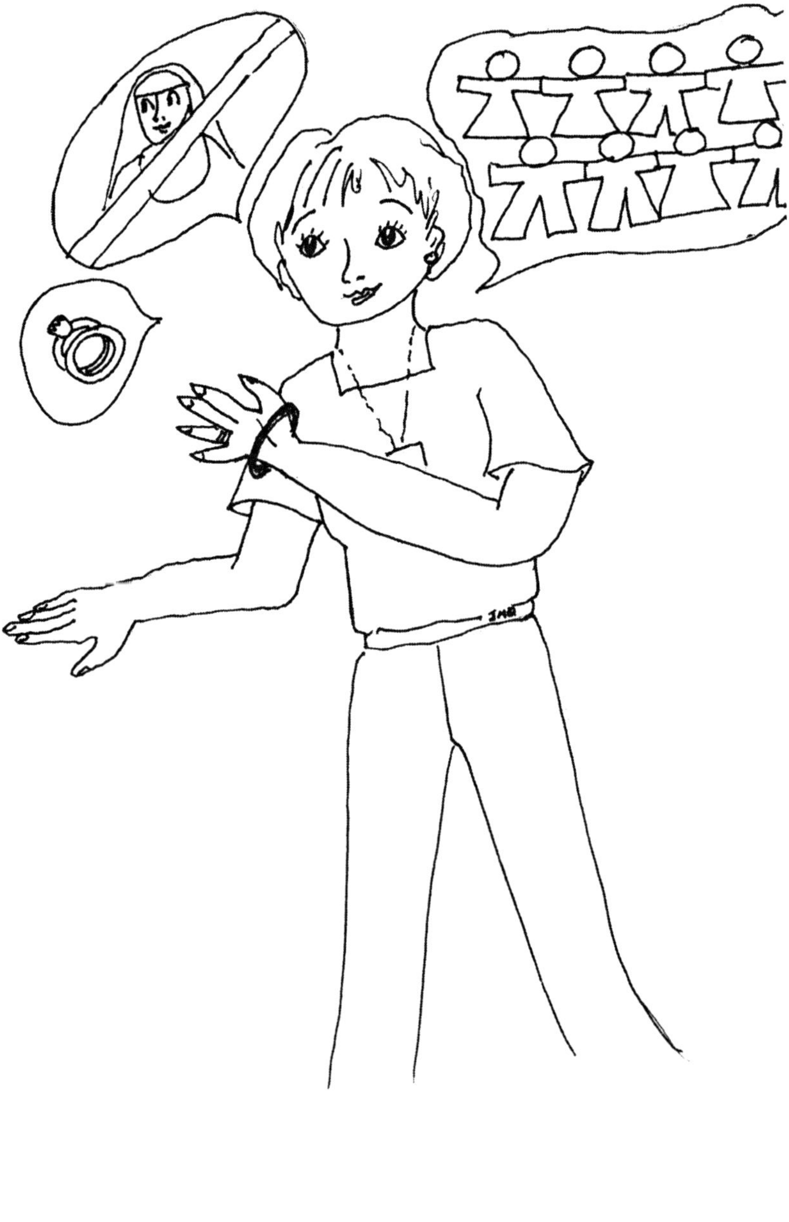

TITLES

From the first day I began to work at the kitchen,
I was called Miss Joanne.
After my boss introduced me that way,
the name stuck.
I was uncomfortable with the Miss part.
Just call me Joanne, I begged.
And besides, I am married a long time away from "Miss".
But no one would cooperate.
Even after eight or nine years I still was tagged with Missy Joanne.
I'd ask a new client,
"How do you want to be called?"
They would say, "first names are best."
There was an innate respect for elders,
especially grandparents.
I admired that.
But at the time I didn't qualify for that venerable category.

In fact, once in awhile I was called Sister.
Well, sure, I am not a religious, but I am the big sis to seven,
but I don't need a handle to remind me or them where I stand.
I was told it is a southern thing,
an African American politeness,
a throw back to when it was demanded.
I am still called by that moniker,
squirming all the way.

Head Day

HARD DAY IN THE PLAYPEN

A lot of people asked,
"Why on earth do you work in a soup kitchen?"
"Not me! I want to see results from my work!"
"Homeless people make me uncomfortable."
"I don't feel sorry for them. They did it to themselves!"
Where else can you find life in its raw essence?
It's a place where hunger cannot be satiated.
The people who come here are clutched in the talons of poverty.
Statistic-ed to death.
No one knows better than they how they got here!
Tomes can cite chapter and verse.
But what good will it do
When people bellow on the radio
"The homeless should be euthanized!"
True, you have to look beyond the blustering noise,
the earthy, human smells
and the tough talk.
The coping skills are incredible here.
The defenses against every indignity known to man saturate the neighborhood.

The choice of anesthetics come in loathsome varieties.
Yes.
It takes strength to slog through a day of horror.
Kiddies can't walk to school without fear of losing their lunch money.
Old ladies hide weapons under their sweaters.
Old men walk fast for fear of the "slicks".
I can't say why I stay.
I can't say why I do it.
But it is a galvanizing place to be.
I know for sure it isn't because of what I give them.
They give me far more.
I am richer for being with the people of the Kitchen.
I witness!

Thanksgiving in the Soup Kitchen

THANKSGIVING IN THE SOUP KITCHEN

It never ceased to amaze me.
It was such a privilege to witness
the private moment
when our dinner guests said grace.
Leaning over their simple plate,
oblivious to the fuss around them,
they closed their eyes.
With worldly possessions plopped at their feet,
I witnessed such dignity and beauty,
as they bowed their heads
low.
Hands open.
Palms up.
Merci, Lord,
For them!

Battered
women's
shelter

BATTERED WOMEN'S SHELTER

There it stood, pale and strange.
Designed like the architect's computer
had a bug in it.
Maybe it was part of the plan to paint it aqua
and have weird angles and strange windows.
Maybe it was meant to be so unattractive
that nobody paid attention.
But to the women who huddled there,
it was their sanctuary from violence and vulnerability.

THE DONOR

The phone jangled during serving time.
"Just what is your criteria for people eating in your soup kitchen?"
the potential donor demanded.
"Be willing to stand in line."
"Be willing to take what's served."
"Is that all?" He growled.
Who would come to the hole in the wall,
endure the impersonal line,
be crushed and huddled for minutes on end
to get a free meal
if he didn't have to?
The staff at the soup kitchen tried
to make the environment
accepting and comfortable,
but it's still hard on anybody's dignity.
You try to make $135.00 a month cover all your family's food!
Sometimes go without income for six months a year!
Work for minimum wage in a god-awful trench job!
Culture of poverty.
Vicious circle!

Whatever the caption.
What I see isn't that.
It's a striving for independence.
It's a mourning for the entrenchment.
"What's happ'ning to us, Sister?"
a diner said to me one morning.
"So many of us black men usin' the soup kitchens, drop-in's!"
"We need a new leader!" he wept.
I wished I could add as I hung up the phone . . . .
Here's part of your answer, sir:
"There's no free lunch!"

Part Five

AMEN. ALLELUIA?

A soup kitchen is not, should not, be a permanent destination. Not for the clients, not for the staff. Ultimately, perhaps a touch altruistic, we would love to drum ourselves out of business.

Kenny Rogers sang, "You know when to hold em, and know when to fold em." And that's how it was with me. Like Antonio, I had the scars to prove my tenure at the kitchen. We all did. Burns, carpel tunnel, frozen shoulders, the beat goes on. In addition to being at the kitchen, the cumulative burdens and challenges of going to school, doing field work, homework, papers, a thesis, some health problems, I thought it would be a good point to move on. I knew it was time to hang my hat. My partner had already left to start her own business. The kitchen was moving to an expanded facility, a old grocery store a few blocks away. The program needed someone in one piece. A fresh face would be a healthy way to start in the new space.

Doing social work there was not like building a house. Seeing the fruit of our labor was rare. We could only hope that the reason why we didn't see the client come through the line anymore was that the client's life improved. I did wonder if any of the services I offered straightened the path on someone's life journey? Did any of the support and "tools" improve conditions for them? Was I really able to quench someone's need?

Did I give our people hope? Victor Hugo said the word which God has written on the brow of every man is *Hope*. I hope what I did in those years was meaningful. I hope it was enough.   jmq

*Thank you for all you
have did for me.
I hope you and your family
has a nice Christmas
and a Grate New Year.*
God bless.

References

Cincinnati Enquirer, *Bill Would Cut Some Ex-con Sanctions*, From Dayton Daily News, 4/27/12

Cincinnati Enquirer, *72 Already Looking for Refuge at Shelter*, By Mark Curnutte, 12/7/11, pg.1B,

Cincinnati Enquirer, Ohio Government, *Holes Growing in Safety Net*, By Paul E. Kostyu, P. B4, 5/27/12

Cincinnati Enquirer, *Increasing Dropouts Draining State's Economy*, By Andrew Benson, Harold Brown, 5/27/12

Cincinnati Enquirer, *Racial Health Gap Persists*, By Mark Curnutte and Mark Wert, 5/26/12

Homes Not Handcuffs: The Criminalization of Homeless in U. S. Cities, Report by the National Law Center on Homelessness and Poverty and the National Coalition for the Homeless, July 2009, PP. 1-194

Med Page Today, *Homelessness Ups Death Risk*, By Michael Smith, North American Correspondent, Published June 14, 2011

STEPPING OUT, On the Pathway to Your Dreams, By Pam Farrell, P. 51, Harvest House Publisher, Eugene, Oregon, 1999

www.bing.com quote of Steven Wright, Pg.1

www.brainyquotes.com, quote of Henry David Thoreau, Pg. 6

www.chipindy/facts.com
Coalition for Homeless Intervention & Prevention.

www.cincihomeless.org/content/hfacts
Greater Cincinnati Coaltion for the Homeless local statistics

www.Cincinnaticoc.org/docs/2006 Continuum of Care for Homeless, Coalition for the Homeless, demographics, count in Cincinnati and Hamilton County.

www.closing the healthgap/org/health
Center for Closing the Gap, racial, ethnic health disparities.

www.endhomelessness.org/about homelessness

National Alliance to End Homelessness
Executive Summary, 3 pages.
www.endhomelessness.org/content/article/detail 1659
National Alliance to End Homelessness, Fact Sheet "Unaccompanied and Homeless Youth, Review of Literature 1995-2005, By Arthur Moore, National Center for Homeless Education.
www.healthfoundation.org/health
Greater Cincinnati Community Health Status Survey by UC Institute of Policy Research, 2010.
www.homelessresourcecenter.samhsa.gov
Fact sheets, statistics.
www.homelessness.samhsa.gov/resource/out of reach 2006
National Low Income Housing Coalition Out of Reach study.
www.mindfully.org/Reform/Dec. 19, 2005
U.S. Conference of Mayors Hunger and Homeless Survey.
www.nationalhomeless.org/factsheets
National Coalition for the Homeless, 3/21/12, 12/15/11, 8/07, 2/21/12.
Statistics, elderly, mental illness, hunger, legislation, employment, addiction, youth, veterans.
www.ncbi.nim.nih.gov
Mental Health: Culture, Race and Ethnicity – A Supplement to Mental Health: A Report of the Surgeon General,1999, Rockville, MD., US Dept. of Health and Human Services, Substance Abuse and Mental Health Services, Administration Center for Mental Health Services, PP. 1-204
www.PBS.ORG/NOW
Facts and Figures on the Homeless, 6/26/09.
www.quotation page.com/quote 571
Quote of John Lennon.
www.socialworkpolicy.org/research/homelessness
www.usich.gov
US Interagency Council on Homeless fact sheets.
www.usingenglish.com/political humor.com
Attributed quotations.
www.usich.gov/opening_doors (US Interagency Council on Homeless)
National Reentry Resource Center.org, federal strategic plan to prevent and end homelessness, 2010.
www.va.gov/homeless
Veterans Administration policy and services to homeless veterans.

CPSIA information can be obtained at www.ICGtesting.com
Printed in the USA
BVOW011644080912

299789BV00003BA/1/P